BOUNDARIES
FOR THRIVING:
LIVING A FULL LIFE
BY SETTING GODLY
BOUNDARIES

Dr. Michael Maiden

Joshua Generation Publishing

BOUNDARIES FOR THRIVING: Living a Full Life by Setting Godly Boundaries

Copyright © 2018

by Dr. Michael Maiden

ISBN-13: 978-1723219214
ISBN-10: 1723219215

Published by
Joshua Generation Publishing
6225 N. Central Ave.
Phoenix, AZ 85012

CONTENTS

INTRODUCTION
BOUNDARIES FOR THRIVING

"Boundaries aren't all bad. That's why there are walls around mental institutions."
- Peggy Noonan

In all seriousness, everyone of us need to learn to set boundaries in our lives. If we want to live God-honoring, thriving lives, we have to be willing to put up Godly boundaries.

There is nothing unloving or un-Christlike for setting healthy, Biblically-based boundaries. Boundaries are a part of anything that works, anything that is successful, anything that is orderly and anything that is healthy. Boundaries are the recognition of personal space.

Throughout this book we will explore what those boundaries are and why we desperately need them in regards to:

- Our identities in Christ
- Truly helping others will staying healthy ourselves
- Dealing with unhealthy leaders and bosses

- Staying pure in a culture that is saturated in immorality
- Dealing with witchcraft and rebellion
- Ungodly and godly soul ties
- Renewing our lives with our words
- And more.

My hope and prayer is that we all learn to thrive in the short period of time we have on this earth. I pray, along with the Apostle John when he wrote to his friend, Gaius:

> "Beloved, I pray that you may prosper in all things and be in health, just as your soul prospers. For I rejoiced greatly when brethren came and testified of the truth that is in you, just as you walk in the truth. I have no greater joy than to hear that my children walk in truth." (3 John 1:2-4)

We can enjoy lives of where our souls prosper.
We can live in health.
We should be living destiny-filled lives.
And we can do so as we learn to walk in the truth of Godly boundaries.
When we set boundaries and learn to say "no" to things that do not contribute to the call of God on our lives, we will find our lives thriving as we have only dared dream possible.

Dr. Michael Maiden
July 2018

CHAPTER ONE
THE GREAT IMPORTANCE OF SETTING HEALTHY BOUNDARIES IN LIFE

"'No' is a complete sentence."
— Anne Lamott

I want to launch into this topic with a startling, life giving, time saving bit of wisdom. It is okay to say, "No."

This notion can change our lives. We must learn that it is okay to set limits and boundaries. There is nothing unloving or un-Christlike for setting healthy, Biblically-based boundaries with other people. Peggy Noonan jokes, "Boundaries aren't all bad. That's why there are walls around mental institutions." Seriously, boundaries are a part of anything that works, anything that is successful, anything that is orderly and anything that is healthy. "Boundaries are, in simple terms, the recognition of personal space." Throughout the word of God, we see God setting boundaries. In the book of Job He asked:

> "Where were you when I laid the foundations of the earth?

Tell Me, if you have understanding.
Who determined its measurements?
Surely you know!
Or who stretched the line upon it?
To what were its foundations fastened?
Or who laid its cornerstone,
When the morning stars sang together,
And all the sons of God shouted for joy?
"Or who shut in the sea with doors,
When it burst forth and issued from the womb;
When I made the clouds its garment,
And thick darkness its swaddling band;
When I fixed My limit for it,
And set bars and doors;
When I said,
'This far you may come, but no farther,
And here your proud waves must stop!'"
(Job 38:4-11)

Rivers flow in between river banks. The oceans stop at the shore. If there weren't river banks or ocean depths, if there wasn't a place for water to be contained, our whole planet would flood.

God created boundaries for day and night. There is always another day, morning and night. God never lets a winter last forever—unless you live in Antarctica. Every season has to relent its grip. Boundaries are a part of God's creative design for the natural world.

This means that boundaries are a part of God's creative design for mankind as well. Healthy people have established healthy boundaries—it's the only way to have a balanced life.

Jesus set boundaries. A great example of this is found in Mark chapter 5.

> Now when Jesus had crossed over again by boat to the other side, a great multitude gathered to Him; and He was by the sea. And behold, one of the rulers of the synagogue came, Jairus by name. And when he saw Him, he fell at His feet and begged Him earnestly, saying, "My little daughter lies at the point of death. Come and lay Your hands on her, that she may be healed, and she will live." So Jesus went with him…While He was still speaking, some came from the ruler of the synagogue's house who said, "Your daughter is dead. Why trouble the Teacher any further?"
>
> As soon as Jesus heard the word that was spoken, He said to the ruler of the synagogue, "Do not be afraid; only believe." And He permitted no one to follow Him except Peter, James, and John the brother of James. Then He came to the house of the ruler of the synagogue, and saw a tumult and those who wept and wailed loudly. When He came in, He said to them, "Why make this commotion and weep? The child is not dead, but sleeping."
>
> And they ridiculed Him. But when He had put them all outside, He took the father and the mother of the child, and those who were with Him, and entered where the child was lying. Then He took the child by the hand, and said to her, "Talitha, cumi," which is translated, "Little girl, I say to you, arise." Immediately the girl arose

and walked, for she was twelve years of age. And they were overcome with great amazement. But He commanded them strictly that no one should know it, and said that something should be given her to eat. (Mark 5:21-24, 35-43)

On the way to Jairus's house, they found out that the daughter was dead. Everyone was beside themselves. Jairus's house filled with mourners to grieve the girls' passing. But Jesus saw another possibility. He saw that the child was not dead, but sleeping. A miracle was in the works. For this to happen, Jesus had to remove people who were in direct opposition to God's will. He came to the house and it was surrounded and full of professional mourners, those paid to grieve the passing of a loved one. Jesus walked in and challenged them. Instantly, their mood changed. They went from being sad, to being mad. They ridiculed Him. A religious spirit rose up against Him.

How did Jesus handle this? Once the spirit was identified, He removed the people Himself. It wasn't that He didn't love them, no, He couldn't do what He was called to with people who were unhealthy, toxic and religious minded standing in the way against Him. He had to move them out, so heaven can move in. He had to set boundaries, and keep unbelief out of the house, so that belief could open the way for the miracle.

Jesus knew the life of the girl was too important to allow detractors direct access. When we are fighting for our marriage, or another person's physical health, or for a business breakthrough, there are some people we can't afford to allow on the inside track of our lives. Their influence is too strong. We don't have enough strength to fight the battle in front of us as well as their influence. Sometimes in life, we have to whittle down the people around us.

Jesus knew this and the result was a little girl being raised from the dead. He showed us that to step into our breakthrough, our miracle, our blessing, there comes a time of separation from others.

In Genesis 13, Abraham and Lot separated and the promise of God came immediately afterwards to Abraham.

> Lot also, who went with Abram, had flocks and herds and tents. Now the land was not able to support them, that they might dwell together, for their possessions were so great that they could not dwell together. And there was strife between the herdsmen of Abram's livestock and the herdsmen of Lot's livestock. The Canaanites and the Perizzites then dwelt in the land.
>
> So Abram said to Lot, "Please let there be no strife between you and me, and between my herdsmen and your herdsmen; for we are brethren. Is not the whole land before you? Please separate from me. If you take the left, then I will go to the right; or, if you go to the right, then I will go to the left."
>
> And the Lord said to Abram, after Lot had separated from him: "Lift your eyes now and look from the place where you are—northward, southward, eastward, and westward; for all the land which you see I give to you and your descendants forever. And I will make your descendants as the dust of the earth; so that if a man could number the dust of the earth, then your descendants also could be numbered. Arise,

walk in the land through its length and its width, for I give it to you."

Then Abram moved his tent, and went and dwelt by the terebinth trees of Mamre, which are in Hebron, and built an altar there to the Lord. (Genesis 13:5-9, 14-18)

Right after Lot had separated from him, Abraham was promised all the land he could see. God could finally talk to Abraham about his future because the one person hindering him was finally removed from his life. God had told Abraham to get away from his family in Genesis 12, but part of his family had come with him. Once Lot was removed, God could step in. Not every person in our life today is going to be with us tomorrow. Some people aren't going where we are going. They have to leave before we can get the next assignment from God.

This can be hard. If God tells us to leave them, or He takes them out of our life, we don't need them. We need to be willing to disengage our emotions from those who are leaving. We don't want them to go because we love them, but God is removing them so we can move on. Our future is more important than soul ties that can't benefit our destiny. Abraham didn't disown Lot. He just separated himself geographically. He didn't kick him out of his family, he just put some distance between the two families.

We are called to love everyone, all the time, but we also need to discern and decide who is to be in our lives, and who we are to be close to. There are those you are called to love, but you are called to love them from afar. Christ had hundreds of followers, seventy plus leaders, twelve disciples, but He had an inner circle of three: James, John and Peter. Not everyone had the same proximity to Christ that these three did. Not everyone had the same access as the twelve did. There were different levels of engagement Christ initiated.

I thank God for my wife. She is magnificent at setting boundaries for our family. I am terrible at it, so she fills in the gap. There are many times when she will need to step in during a service, or a meeting, to help me set boundaries with those coming for ministry. Often she will send me a note or comes and get me because she is discerning that I need to disengage from a meeting or ministry time. I have allowed the boundaries to dissolve, and the benefit of the moment is gone.

We must be able to recognize the people in our lives that drain us. There are people that come into our world and steal the momentum from our life because they need it for their life. Instead of living off their own faith, they are using ours. We can carry people like that for a while. But there comes a time when the relationship becomes so uneven, it costs us too much. When we see relationships impacting our marriage or home or business in a negative manner, it is time to do something about it. If we are being drained emotionally and physically we have to make a quality decision, and lovingly set boundaries.

COMMITMENT & IDENTITY

Often, in the gospel of John, he makes brief, powerful, insightful statements that, if we aren't careful, we overlook. In John 2:24, he says, "But Jesus did not commit Himself to them, because He knew all men..." This one little phrase says so much.

First, we learn that our level of commitment to people needs to be determined by the level of commitment they make to us. Leaders, we cannot commit to people that won't submit. That doesn't mean we tell people where to work, who to marry, where to live, but submission is a biblical truth and a condition of the heart. If God calls someone to follow us, and He speaks to us, that person needs to be willing to receive the word God has spoken.

Secondly, we need to take time to understand people and how they work. Christ knew people because He was a student of human nature. He knew what people wanted most of all: acceptance. He understood the need we have for acceptance is one of the key areas the enemy targets. One of the enemy's most effective tactics is to try and keep us in unhealthy engagements out of fear of rejection. Jesus didn't need people to tell Him who He was or to add value to His life. A problem arises if a platform, ministry, stage, a job, or any position becomes our primary source of meeting our identity needs. If it overrides God's message of our importance, then we create a codependency on people or things. This will inhibit relationships and growth in all areas. Read John 2:23-25 in the Message translation:

> During the time he was in Jerusalem, those days of the Passover Feast, many people noticed the signs he was displaying and, seeing they pointed straight to God, entrusted their lives to him. But Jesus didn't entrust his life to them. He knew them inside and out, knew how untrustworthy they were. He didn't need any help in seeing right through them.

People have agendas. Some are stronger than others. Jesus understood unhealthy agendas. The Holy Spirit will help us in our daily lives to discern the wrong agendas people have and are trying to trap us into. "If you fear that defending your boundaries is being controlling, don't worry. There is a difference between being controlling and having boundaries. Controlling people is about telling them what to do. Setting boundaries is about saying what you do or do not want to happen to you." We just have to listen to and follow the Spirit's lead.

OTHER PEOPLE'S STORMS

Some of the spiritual warfare we are engaged in isn't caused by us. Some of the spiritual warfare we face is because someone else in our life is in a storm. After awhile, there will be so much water in our boat, we will have to make a decision to go down with them, or toss them overboard. We have to be strong enough to say "no" to protect our family and our own health. I learned this long ago after reading and studying Jonah's story.

> Now the word of the Lord came to Jonah the son of Amittai, saying, "Arise, go to Nineveh, that great city, and cry out against it; for their wickedness has come up before Me." But Jonah arose to flee to Tarshish from the presence of the Lord. He went down to Joppa, and found a ship going to Tarshish; so he paid the fare, and went down into it, to go with them to Tarshish from the presence of the Lord.

But the Lord sent out a great wind on the sea, and there was a mighty tempest on the sea, so that the ship was about to be broken up.

Then the mariners were afraid; and every man cried out to his god, and threw the cargo that was in the ship into the sea, to lighten the load. But Jonah had gone down into the lowest parts of the ship, had lain down, and was fast asleep.

So the captain came to him, and said to him, "What do you mean, sleeper? Arise, call on your God; perhaps your God will consider us, so that we may not perish."

And they said to one another, "Come, let us cast lots, that we may know for whose cause this trouble has come upon us." So they cast lots, and the lot fell on Jonah. Then they said to him, "Please tell us! For whose cause is this trouble upon us? What is your occupation? And where do you come from? What is your country? And of what people are you?"

So he said to them, "I am a Hebrew; and I fear the Lord, the God of heaven, who made the sea and the dry land."

Then the men were exceedingly afraid, and said to him, "Why have you done this?" For the men knew that he fled from the presence of the Lord, because he had told them. Then they said to him, "What shall we do to you that the sea may be calm for us?"—for the sea was growing more tempestuous.

And he said to them, "Pick me up and throw me into the sea; then the sea will become calm for you. For I know that this great tempest is because of me."

Nevertheless the men rowed hard to return to land, but they could not, for the sea continued to grow more tempestuous against them. Therefore they cried out to the Lord and said, "We pray, O Lord, please do not let us perish for this man's life, and do not charge us with innocent blood; for You, O Lord, have done as it pleased You." So they picked up Jonah and threw him into the sea, and the sea ceased from its raging. Then the men feared the Lord exceedingly, and offered a sacrifice to the Lord and took vows. (Jonah 1:1-16)

Jonah had a mission, but he turned it down. He ran from it. He went in the exact opposite direction from where God sent him. There was one main reason: the Jewish people had enmity against the Syrians. The Syrians were massively cruel to Israel. God wanted Jonah to prophesy a second chance to his arch enemy. Jonah's prejudices rose up and he ran from God. The moment he ran, he created a storm and it almost cost other people their lives.

Someone out there is in the midst of a raging storm in their life. And it isn't their fault. Someone else has caused it. One person in an active storm can cause havoc for a whole group of people. We all need to learn this life altering truth: never let someone else's storm destroy your life.

There are some people that are so damaging in our world, that we have to let them go. We have to toss them into the arms of God. God's arms are big enough to handle the rebel in our family. He is big enough to handle the person that is causing all kinds of disruptions in our homes. Sometimes we have to take a step back, and let God take over. Stop trying to fix people that don't want to be fixed.

This is hard to do. The professional sailors, nonbelievers, were terrified of Jonah's storm, and the captain found Jonah in the bottom of the boat, asleep. Everyone was more concerned about the storm than he was. Yet, even after Jonah's admission, these sailors didn't want to toss him overboard. They had no choice, their lives were on the line.

When Jonah exposed his running, the men were really terrified. They realized that a God that could cause this storm was massive and powerful. We can be so selfishly engaged in our indulgent self pity, while people's lives around us are being ruined, that we hardly notice it. A whole group of men were going to die because one person had a storm in his life. It's really hard to help people that don't want help. It's a tough thing when a whole family is upset, but the person that needs help isn't."Wisdom is better than weapons of war; But one sinner destroys much good." (Ecc. 9:18)

JUST SAY NO

"Establishing clear boundaries is a necessary part of living an authentic life. And only you get to decide what your boundaries are. It's important to have boundaries, and to be clear about what they are. Let others know what is okay, and what is not okay for you."
— *Scott Stabile*

It's healthy for children to learn to say "no" in life. It is good that a child learn to set boundaries. A baby can't distinguish itself from its mother. After four to five months, a child's personality emerges and behavior, independent of mother, grows and grows and grows. Then they come to the "no" stage. It might be hard at first, but we have to realize it's okay for kids to go through this phase. They have to know they can set boundaries. It's okay to say "no." People that can't say no will always end up in traumatic, toxic environments. We have to learn to say "no," again, as adults. In fact, we have to learn to say "no," stepping back from people with control issues and the inability to say "no" themselves.

People that really love us, want us to be healthy and establish parameters of engagement with other people. When I first started pastoring, early morning prayer was in our house at 5:30am. Our kids would wake up and wander around into the prayer time in their pajamas. I learned, with my wife, to protect our family from an unbalanced and unhealthy relationship with the church. I didn't want my kids growing up with an attitude against the church because the church stole us away from them.

Several times in Christ's life, the crowds grew so big that they were called multitudes. Frequently there were thousands of people in front of Him, and He would turn to His disciples, and say, we have to go. He would walk away from amazingly large crowds. I don't know many modern day preachers that would do that, but He knew and understood when the level of engagement had reached a point where it was too depleting, and it would hurt Him to stay with the crowd. He would withdraw and go to the mountain to pray and replenish. There, He resupplied His energy, His faith, and His love. It was there that He would get more so He could give more.

In the western world, Americans are known as taking the least amount of vacations. When I was a young pastor, I used to foolishly brag about not taking vacations. I was proud of the fact that I was at my church year 'round, preaching, serving, and ministering all the time. I then realized, as I grew a little older, that was a dumb thing to brag about. I want to reiterate this point: healthy people know when to pull back. They know when to take care of themselves. They know when to replenish their souls. They know that it's okay to disengage.

DON'T SACRIFICE YOUR LIFE
TO PACIFY UNHEALTHY PEOPLE

Christians are the most loving people on earth. I see this on a daily basis in my own life. The members of my church are constant examples of how we are to live the gospel. They are loving on people twenty-four hours a day in practical, Biblical ways: counseling them, feeding them, praying for them. I am proud of their efforts, and I encourage them to keep going.

I am also encouraging them to know when to say when. In over forty years of ministry, I have seen more than a fair share of wonderful, well-meaning, good-hearted people get burned by those they are helping simply because they had not set boundaries. "When you notice someone does something toxic the first time, don't wait for the second time before you address it or cut them off. Many survivors are used to the 'wait and see' tactic which only leaves them vulnerable to a second attack. As your boundaries get stronger, the wait time gets shorter. You never have to justify your intuition." (Shahida Arabi)

Here is one example I see quite often. We all know someone that is what I call the "Constantly Angry Person." These are toxic people. They are the kind of person we can calm down for the moment, but the anger will always come back. Proverbs 19:19 says:

> "A man of great wrath will suffer punishment;
> For if you rescue him, you will have to do it
> again."

I have seen this type of person ruin marriages over and over again. The wife is unwilling to cut loose that angry husband who is physically or emotionally abusing her. She loves him and wants God to change him. Often, I will tell them that in the Christian faith, nothing says they have to stay with an abusive person. They—and we—need to realize that God has not called us to pacify unhealthy people. He doesn't want us to sacrifice our health for those that won't receive the help.

We all have people in our extended families that we have to protect ourselves and our families from because they are toxic. That doesn't mean that we stop praying for them, or loving them. It means that we stay away because their storms will destroy our lives. In my life, I keep coming back to this same truth: I have a enough battles to fight, I don't need their fight as well.

By looking at Jesus and how He handled people, we can see what an amazing radar He had when it came to discerning what was in people's hearts. We can see how He went about protecting himself from them. Here's the key in His life: He listened to and obeyed the Holy

Spirit. Here's the good news: the same Holy Spirit that was in Christ is in us. He will help us establish healthy relationships.

Our future depends on boundaries. I Corinthians 15:33 says, "Do not be deceived: 'Evil company corrupts good habits.'" If we aren't winning people over for Christ, they are winning us over to the world's system. If we aren't strong enough in our walk with Christ, we will soon find ourselves acting like those we are trying to help. And they will not be acting like us, like Christ. That doesn't mean we don't befriend those that don't believe in Christ. We need to shine our lights into their worlds. We cannot become ensnared in their sinful behavior. We have to watch out for times when we start getting pulled away from God. Anybody in our world that pulls us away from God, we have to separate from them or put up boundaries.

Why? Our futures depend on it. I can tell where someone's future lies by the friends they hang out with. Our friends are a prophesy of our future. Yes, we need to have some people in our lives that need Christ. But if we aren't winning them, we are losing. Paul says that we should "note those who cause divisions and offenses, contrary to the doctrine which you learned, and avoid them." (Romans 16:17) Paul doesn't tell us to curse these people or throw them to the devil. He says to avoid them. Proverbs tells us, "Make no friendship with an angry man, and with a furious man do not go, lest you learn his ways and set a snare for your soul." (Proverbs 22:24-25)

If we befriend an angry man, we will become an angry man because people like this carry offenses, bitterness, and agendas. They want us to become like them, to adopt their view of things so they can feel validated. We need to be careful how much input they have in our life. We must measure how much of them we can handle before their offense passes on to our souls.

"The most basic boundary-setting word is "no." It lets others know that we exist apart from them and that we are in control of ourselves."
— Dr. Henry Cloud & Dr. John Townsend

CHAPTER TWO
WHEN HELPING OTHERS
IS HURTING YOU

When we fail to set boundaries and hold people accountable,
we feel used and mistreated.
This is why we sometimes attack who they are,
which is far more hurtful than addressing a behavior or a
choice.
- Brene Brown

God wants all of us to function in this world and remain healthy in His kingdom. God wants us to be able to love people and survive encounters with unhealthy people. He has given us the tools to take care of ourselves so we can help others without destroying our own life. Why? Jesus loves toxic people. He loves unhealthy people. He loves people that have either emotional or mental or personality issues that drive them to behave in un-Christlike ways. We are called to love them and to survive them. That is why we have the Spirit of God who fills us with God's love for them.

This idea of loving those who are hard to love is what drives my ministry. I have the honor of working with thousands of pastors all over the world. The occupation of being a pastor means you are emotionally vulnerable, which causes it to be a dangerous occupation. The older I've gotten, the more I have focused on the singular issue of helping ministers remain healthy by learning to both love and survive the toxic people in our churches. This means setting boundaries and maintaining them. This means dealing with controlling people. This means doing the necessary work of caring for ourselves.

These notions aren't just for pastors. I want these lessons to get out into the body at large. We all have to learn to set boundaries for those people who are damaged and invading our space. We have to take better care of ourselves. We cannot help others if we are not first helping ourselves.

KEEP AN EYE ON YOUR GAUGES

They are some things that are vital to helping us stay healthy. The first one comes down to this: Don't Burnout. If we keep our car engines running when it is out of oil, we will burn the engine out. We know that we should never drive our car when the gauge says the oil is running low. The same goes for our own lives. When we are running low on the oil or anointing of God, we will burn out. God wants us to learn to read our gauges. He gives us these protective instruments so that we know when we have to go to Him for a refill.

One sign that we are close to burn out is when our outtake exceeds our intake. When we spend more of our time pouring into others than we do allowing God to pour into us, something in our life is going to break. We all have seasons, or relationships, or events when we are constantly being depleted. But that shouldn't be the norm. We cannot get to the place where we are not able to replenish our emotional, spiritual and mental energies regularly. If we do, eventually our soul, mind and body will have some kind of breech.

Jesus understood this. We can often see that after ministering to multitudes of people, suddenly, without cause or reason, he would turn his back, grab his disciples and go away to pray. What was he doing? Recharging his batteries: he knew if he kept running and giving on empty, he would burn out. Christ wants us to follow his example. We need to get away and allow the Holy Spirit to fill us up again.

> Therefore He says:
> "Awake, you who sleep,
> Arise from the dead,
> And Christ will give you light."
> See then that you walk circumspectly, not as fools but as wise, 16 redeeming the time, because the days are evil.
> Therefore do not be unwise, but understand what the will of the Lord is. And do not be drunk with wine, in which is dissipation; but be filled with the Spirit, speaking to one another in psalms and hymns and spiritual songs, singing and making melody in your heart to the Lord, 20 giving thanks always for all things to God the Father in the name of our Lord Jesus Christ, 21 submitting to one another in the fear of God. (Eph. 5:14-21)

God's will is for the Holy Spirit to be such a presence in our lives, that he affects our emotions, our thoughts, and our feelings. When we think of the fruit of the spirit—"love, joy, peace, longsuffering, kindness, goodness, faithfulness, gentleness, self-control" (Gal. 5:22)—we need to see that six of those nine things are emotionally related. The Holy Spirit is the one that empowers and enables our emotions to overcome the stresses and strains that this world puts upon us. We can go to the Holy Spirit everyday and ask Him to fill us with His love for people. Why? Yesterdays love isn't enough for today. How? Ephesians 5 tells us to speak to ourselves in "psalms and hymns and spiritual songs, singing and making melody in your heart to the Lord, giving thanks always for all things to God the Father in the name of our Lord Jesus Christ, submitting to one another in the fear of God." (5:19-21)

I love this. I love worship because it replenishes our soul by connecting us to God. He recharges our batteries and refills our tank. David said that God was His Shepherd who was working to restore His soul. He talked about encounters with God among peaceful waters and beautiful pastures. In the midst of lovingly shepherding us, the Holy Spirit is restoring our souls.

Working with people, living with people, dealing with people on a daily basis can feel overwhelming. But we have hope. God knows how to fix what others have broken inside us. He knows how to replenish us. No matter how we feel about the people in our world, God can give us the capacity by His Spirit to love everybody, all the time.

Alongside being filled with the Spirit to keep our engines running, we need to make sure not to neglect the tools and resources God has put into our lives. "Do not neglect the gift that is in you, which was given to you by prophecy with the laying on of the hands of the eldership. Meditate on these things; give yourself entirely to them, that your progress may be evident to all. Take heed to yourself and to the doctrine. Continue in them, for in doing this you will save both yourself and those who hear you." (1 Timothy 4:14-15) Paul, in writing to his spiritual son, Timothy, gives us valuable, life-saving advice. Paul tells us that whenever we neglect our gift that is to be a tool or resource for us, we are in trouble. Any are that falls into neglect, gets worse. The law of corruption in nature is that anything left to itself gets worse.

We have to maintain our garden, maintain our house, maintain our life. We have to care for ourselves and our gifts. It is time to stop neglecting the treasures God has given us. He has downloaded into us everything we need to do what He has called us to do. God's put everything in us that we need to fulfill our destiny. Our gifts are capable of fulfilling our calling. God gives us what we need to get to the end of our road. God wants us to think about the gifts and resources He has given us by his Spirit and his Word. We are to mediate on, think about and prioritize those things so that will grow us spiritually and emotionally.

God doesn't want us getting sick while we make others better. We have to pay attention to ourselves as human beings. This is not selfish. This is not anti-Biblical. Our first responsibility is always to ourselves. This is not often preached from the pulpit. We hear that we are to die to ourself but that's only a partial truth. Our selfishness has to die, yes, but our love has to live. Our fleshy impulses have to die, but our callings and purposes have to live. God wants us to make sure we are paying attention to our love tank, to our gifts and our callings. He wants us to be in tune with and reading the gauges of our life. Physically, our bodies will tell us when we are getting low on spiritual, emotional and mental energy.

This bears repeating until we all grasp this truth: if we are not taking care of ourselves, we can't possibly take care of anyone else. If a mother who is reading this is raising kids, she knows it is a full time job. It can be crazy. You have to get up early to do a thousand things. You will come to the end of yourself if you don't manage things in your own world. You will burn out doing something that you love to do. You have to give yourself breaks and respites. You have to give yourself replenishing moments. You have to monitor your health. It is good to take care of yourself. It is good to yearn for, believe for and practice behaviors that allow for you to be healthy emotionally. You have permission to take care of you.

Don't draw back from what I am saying. Many of us have been taught this is selfish. I am not talking about truly selfish people. I am talking about people that have a hard time saying "no" to anyone. They are running on empty. They are in a situation where their life is issuing a desperate silent cry. They aren't used to listening to their own hearts and, if they aren't careful, they spontaneously break down.

Here is a side note: we have to be on guard for those around us that are always giving. We need to help them monitor their own energy as well. They are not superwoman or superman. They need our help so they don't break down. When I am counseling with pastors, I am always looking for signs of burn out. Lately, a few of my friends have gone on sabbaticals. It's a good thing. They have to take care of themselves. We don't have to do everything. We don't have to be everywhere. We just have to pray about what we should do. We just have to pray about where we need to be. Refuel when you are running low and stop when you are running hot.

DEALING WITH CONTROLLING PEOPLE

In every aspect of our lives, we will encounter strong people—some good, some not so good. We have to learn to work with the Godly ones and deal with the ungodly ones effectively to stay emotionally and spiritually healthy. "Be honest with who you are, what you want and how you want to be treated. Boundaries only scare off the people that were not meant to be in your life." (Shannon L. Alder)

Let me first say, the body of Christ needs strong leaders. A strong person can be a powerful messenger of Christ when God is in control of their lives. We need people with drive, courage and perseverance. All of these traits are positive, but these stallions need to be corralled, bridled and restrained. God wants to help them. God isn't looking to make them weak. He just wants to set them free from the possibility of controlling spirits taking control of their lives through the sin and unhealthy emotional behavior. These are the people we have to learn to work with.

The people we need to deal with by the wisdom and compassion of the Spirit of God are people under the control of a controlling spirit. Controlling people are controlled people. They have unhealthy attitudes living in them. When we see Christ confronting these types of people, He is often confronting people with unclean spirits in them. The devil uses people through controlling spirits to unleash the weapon of oppression on other people.

One way to spot a person with a controlling spirit is that they will never lose an argument. They won't take no for an answer. They won't let you out of an argument. They make every attempt to rule with fear. We often find ourselves afraid of angering them, especially if this type of person is in our family. Everyone says not to push their buttons. Everyone walks around on pins and needles trying not to offend. That person is manipulating others through emotions.

How did they get this way? A controlling spirit found a home there because of the unhealed and unclean aspects of their life. Sinful patterns of life and unhealthy emotions have opened the door to demonic oppression. I am here to say that Christ can help these people get free, but that is not my subject. I want you to know how to identify if you are being attacked by a controlling spirit, how to overcome that attack and how to set boundaries to stop the attacks in the future.

First, let's look at how to identify the attack. I Kings 19 gives us a great picture of what it means to be under attack and oppressed by a controlling spirit in someone's life:

> And Ahab told Jezebel all that Elijah had done, also how he had executed all the prophets with the sword. Then Jezebel sent a messenger to Elijah, saying, "So let the gods do to me, and more also, if I do not make your life as the life of

one of them by tomorrow about this time." And
when he saw that, he arose and ran for his life,
and went to Beersheba, which belongs to Judah,
and left his servant there.

But he himself went a day's journey into the
wilderness, and came and sat down under a
broom tree. And he prayed that he might die, and
said, "It is enough! Now, Lord, take my life, for I
am no better than my fathers!"

Then as he lay and slept under a broom tree,
suddenly an angel touched him, and said to him,
"Arise and eat." Then he looked, and there by
his head was a cake baked on coals, and a jar of
water. So he ate and drank, and lay down again.
7 And the angels of the Lord came back the
second time, and touched him, and said, "Arise
and eat, because the journey is too great for you."
So he arose, and ate and drank; and he went in
the strength of that food forty days and forty
nights as far as Horeb, the mountain of God. (1
Kings 19:1-8)

Before we get into the meat of this passage, I want
to make sure all of the women reading this who are
strong, who have stood up for themselves in the church
world, and who are called Jezebel's for talking a stand,
realize that I am not isolating you. Standing up for
yourself is something that God wants. He wants women
to be strong. He doesn't want them to be controlled or
controlling. I strongly believe that women need to be
empowered in the church. Women are not second class
citizens in the kingdom of God! The fact that Jezebel
is a woman is not the focus. Jezebel is a picture of a
controlling spirit—male or female.

The first thing we need to identify is this: spiritual warfare most commonly comes through words. God created via the word. The spiritual world is governed by words. Negative or positive words are the spiritual weaponry of the spirit world. They are the spiritual resources that accomplish things. Jezebel sent a word that acted as a weapon. Controlling people use words to manipulate, intimidate and dominate people. These people can be our bosses, employees, spouses, friends—it doesn't matter. When someone is trying to manipulate, intimidate or dominate, it will come out in their vocabulary.

Take notice: Jezebel spoke, but Elijah saw. When a controlling spirit in someone speaks, we are the one's that will see or visualize those words and that is how they become a reality. These words get into our souls and have an impact. Here are four rare symptoms that show up when we are in spiritual warfare and/or facing burn out from fighting controlling spirits:

1. The desire to isolate yourself.

When we want to move to the mountains and live in a cave far from anyone else, we are fighting that spirit. When we cut off all communications, we don't want to talk to anyone, this is a sign of burn out/spiritual warfare/controlling spirits. When we get that desire, we have to push back. Do the things we don't want to do. We need to surround ourselves with people the most when we don't want to be with them at all.

2. Unusual physical or emotional exhaustion or fatigue.

This is the type of exhaustion that often comes after a breakthrough for the kingdom of God. Often when it is done, there can be a vulnerable period of weeks or months where we are unusually tired. I am talking about unusual fatigue or exhaustion that seems to come out of nowhere and it overwhelms us. This is a sign of burn out/warfare.

3. Deep discouragement or depression.

This is not a normal type of discouragement. This might seem equal to depression, but it is short lived, it is intense and it is deep. If you are experiencing this, it's not just you. You need more than vitamins. You are in spiritual warfare. There is some kind of controlling power coming against you.

4. Suicidal thoughts. Elijah's admission that he was not better than his father's wasn't bad.

It's good to recognize that we are standing on the shoulders of our forefathers. But hopelessness, despondency, and suicidal thoughts were out of character for Elijah. This was so opposite of his normal world. It's obvious he was under attack. Recognize that suicide is abnormal to our survival instincts that God gave us. It's almost always demonic infused when it comes into our lives. This comes when people are facing burn out, fighting spiritual battles and worn out. This is not a good place to be.

These are signs that we are facing a demonic, controlling spirit. How do we defeat it?

My wife and I started our first church in Scottsdale, Arizona in 1985, after the leaders of the church where I was an associate in California approached me with their plan to fire my father and make me the new senior pastor. I immediately rejected their proposal and my wife and I moved four hundred and thirty-five miles away to start clean and right with God in Phoenix. We had nothing but the word of God. He blessed it. Our church grew. Things were going well.

Then, about a year into it, I felt hopeless, depressed and detached from God. I am prophetic and, if I'm not hearing from God, I have nothing to say. God was not talking to me. I was upset. I was praying and confessing sins. He told me I had done nothing wrong. He showed me I was under spiritual warfare: two pastors had cursed me and said I would fail and was out of God's will. I believed what God was saying to me, but I asked for confirmation. In the following two weeks, people came from those two churches in California and told me what their pastors had publicly said.

During that time, God told me to love them but bind the power of their controlling words against my life. He then lead me to Isaiah 54:17:

> "No weapon formed against you shall prosper,
>   And every tongue which rises against you in judgment
>   You shall condemn.
>   This is the heritage of the servants of the Lord,
>   And their righteousness is from Me,"
>   Says the Lord.

Remember the weapons Satan uses in our lives always begin in word form. I broke every word curse spoken against our lives. You can and should do the same. When I finished praying that verse, I felt heaven come into that room in my heart. I pray that prayer several times a week. I pray blessings for controlling people, out of love and then take authority over and break any curses that have been spoken over me. When we are engaged with controlling people, we have to break the curses against our life.

There are people reading this right now, who have had a controlling parent or spouse that was emotionally detached from them and they said things against you that you have never taken authority over. Take a few moments and pray Isaiah 54:17 over your life. Allow God to deal with those controlling words today and set you free.

Now that we know an important way to break the attacks off of our life, let's look at how we refuel from an attack and establish boundaries to stop future attacks.

Whatever you feed dominates you. Going back to the story of Elijah and Jezebel, we see that the angel fed Elijah two meals. He was being replenished physically, spiritually, emotionally and mentally. Every realm of his life was being restored. God has a diet for us. The word of God is our faith diet. The Bible is the meal that heals. There are so many books out there, but the only book in humanity that has the life and nature of God, is the Bible. When we read the Bible, our spirit man is fed, our emotions come in line, our mental outlook changes and our physical body is healed. We find ourselves recovering from encounters with Jezebel through feeding off the Word of God.

We have to learn to say no to controlling people, or they will bring control into our lives through intimidation, manipulation, or domination. There are so many people that have been worn out by life or discouragement or long term struggles or the engagement of a controlling person, that they've had a hard time saying no. But in Jesus name, God is restoring your will power. He is healing our will power to say no to demonic powers. When people who represent these controlling powers come into our lives, yes we love them, but no, we won't be controlled by them.

The love and grace of Jesus Christ will help us restore the lost ability to say no because of brokenness in our souls. We can recover our will power and find our voice in order to say no to those spirits. We can define healthy boundaries so that our life and our relationships will flourish.

Jesus had control freaks amongst his twelve disciples: James and Peter, for example. He had to set boundaries with both of them. James wanted to be at Jesus' right hand. He wanted a place of power. Jesus set the boundaries with him by saying, "You will indeed drink My cup, and be baptized with the baptism that I am baptized with; but to sit on My right hand and on My left is not Mine to give, but it is for those for whom it is prepared by My Father." (Matthew 20:23) With Peter, He had to use even stronger language. Peter stepped out of line and said something that, well, irked Christ. Christ responded by saying,"Get behind Me, Satan! You are an offense to Me, for you are not mindful of the things of God, but the things of men." (Matthew 16:23) These powerful leaders had to mature and to mature, they had to have lines drawn.

We should never complain about people overstepping boundaries that we have not made known. "Many of us find it hard to set boundaries and defend them because we fear doing so will cause rejection or abandonment. We may avoid confrontations to make things easier. We may feel guilt if we say no or if we think we might hurt someone's feelings. We fear boundaries will keep us from being loved." (Adelyn Birch) But we can't be afraid of setting them, especially with strong people in our lives. Some people around us are just strong leaders. They don't know what they don't know. If you don't communicate the boundaries, they won't know they are overstepping. Set up the boundaries and make them plain. Never complain about what you refuse to confront. Never assume that people know more than what you tell them.

Here are some things we can do to begin establishing boundaries with the strong leader types in families, work, church and elsewhere:

1. Name our limits.

"We can't set good boundaries if we're unsure of where we stand…We should consider what we can tolerate and accept and what makes us feel uncomfortable or stressed. Feelings help us identify what our limits are."

2. Tune into our feelings.

"Two key feelings in others are red flags or cues that we're letting go of our boundaries: discomfort and resentment. During an interaction or in a situation, we can ask ourselves, what is causing that? What is it about this interaction, or the person's expectation that is bothering me? Feeling uncomfortable is a cue to us they may be violating or crossing a boundary."

3. Be direct.

With some people, maintaining healthy boundaries doesn't require a direct and clear-cut dialogue. With others, such as those who have a different personality or cultural background, we'll need to be more direct about our boundaries. Consider the following example: "one person feels [that] challenging someone's opinions is a healthy way of communicating," but to another person this feels disrespectful and tense.

4. Give yourself permission.

Fear, guilt and self-doubt are all something we battle. We might fear the other person's response if we set and enforce our boundaries. We might feel guilty by speaking up or saying no to a family member. Many believe that they should be able to cope with a situation or say yes because they're a good daughter or son, even though they "feel drained or taken advantage of." We might wonder if we even deserve to have boundaries in the first place.

5. Practice self-awareness.

Boundaries are all about honing in on our feelings and honoring them. If we notice ourselves slipping and not sustaining our boundaries ask yourself: What's changed? Consider "What I am doing or [what is] the other person doing?" or "What is the situation eliciting that's making me resentful or stressed?" Then, mull over our options: "What am I going to do about the situation? What do I have control over?"

6. Consider our past and present.

How we were raised along with our role in our families can become additional obstacles in setting and preserving boundaries. If we were the family caretaker, we learned to focus on others, were drained emotionally or physically. Ignoring our own needs might have become the norm for us. It is also vital to think about the people we are surrounded by. Is there a healthy give and take in the relationship?

7. Seek support.

When having a hard time with boundaries, it is good to seek the help of our churches, our friends, our counselors, our pastors. Work with family to help each other set boundaries. We should also consider looking through other resources for help.

8. Be assertive.

It's not enough to create boundaries; we actually have to follow through. Even though we know people can't read our minds, we still expect them to know what causes us pain. People don't unless we tell them. We should be actively communicating with others if they cross a boundary, in a respectful way.

9. Start small.

Practice makes perfect. Communicating our boundaries takes practice. Psychologists suggest beginning with small boundaries, and then incrementally increasing to more challenging boundaries.

BREAK CONTROLLING SPIRITS

I want to end this chapter by saying this: if you are experiencing any of the four symptoms of attack from Elijah's life, please know that there is nothing wrong with you. You are under attack. In fact, you are most likely on the verge of your largest breakthrough. I want you to realize you don't have to stay in that attack. You can be free today. You don't need a preacher to break the devil off of you. Work hard to build your faith on God's word and deepen your relationship with Christ. If you are saved, you have authority to break the controlling spirits power off of you.

I want you to do that now. I want you pray Isaiah 54:17 right now and break those lying, controlling demonic words off your life, and watch as God works.

CHAPTER THREE
SURVIVING UNHEALTHY LEADERS

*"Just as we expect others to value our boundaries,
it's equally important for us to respect the boundaries of
others."*
— *Laurie Buchanan, PhD*

I want to make something very clear at the outset of
this chapter: leadership is God's answer. Most of the
problems we see in the world today are caused by a lack
of good leadership or by the presence of bad leadership.
Time and time again, when history was changed for the
better, it is because someone answered the call of God to
step up and lead in His kingdom. Whenever God is ready
to intervene in a generation, He raises up strong leaders.

Guess what? That is all of us. When we were saved and
born again, we were drafted into the leadership school
called the church. In the church, God forms us to impact
the culture with His kingdom and grace. When God has
something on His mind, when He has something He
wants to do in this world, leaders are the ones who hear
and respond to God's heart and voice.

Having said that, we all need to recognize that leaders are just people. I have come to realize that church leaders are people that have said "yes" to God so many times that God can't say "no" to them. They struggle to stay healthy like all of us. I have been an unhealthy leader before and I am working to make sure I am never unhealthy again.

THINGS THAT DERAILS LEADERS
(AND HOW WE CAN AVOID THEIR MISTAKES)

Setting boundaries that help us survive unhealthy leaders is vital in our walk with Christ and our own development as leaders. Before we can set boundaries with them, we need to recognize how leaders become toxic, so that we can avoid their course, and know how to pray for them. For this study, we will look at the life of Saul, and see how we can avoid his pitfalls.

> Samuel also said to Saul, "The Lord sent me to anoint you king over His people, over Israel. Now therefore, heed the voice of the words of the Lord. Thus says the Lord of hosts: 'I will punish Amalek for what he did to Israel, how he ambushed him on the way when he came up from Egypt. Now go and attack Amalek, and utterly destroy all that they have, and do not spare them. But kill both man and woman, infant and nursing child, ox and sheep, camel and donkey.'"
> So Saul gathered the people together and numbered them in Telaim, two hundred

thousand foot soldiers and ten thousand men of
Judah. And Saul came to a city of Amalek, and lay
in wait in the valley.

Then Saul said to the Kenites, "Go, depart, get
down from among the Amalekites, lest I destroy
you with them. For you showed kindness to all
the children of Israel when they came up out of
Egypt." So the Kenites departed from among the
Amalekites. And Saul attacked the Amalekites,
from Havilah all the way to Shur, which is east of
Egypt. He also took Agag king of the Amalekites
alive, and utterly destroyed all the people with
the edge of the sword. But Saul and the people
spared Agag and the best of the sheep, the oxen,
the fatlings, the lambs, and all that was good,
and were unwilling to utterly destroy them. But
everything despised and worthless, that they
utterly destroyed.

Now the word of the Lord came to Samuel,
saying, "I greatly regret that I have set up Saul
as king, for he has turned back from following
Me, and has not performed My commandments."
And it grieved Samuel, and he cried out to the
Lord all night. So when Samuel rose early in
the morning to meet Saul, it was told Samuel,
saying, "Saul went to Carmel, and indeed, he
set up a monument for himself; and he has gone
on around, passed by, and gone down to Gilgal."
Then Samuel went to Saul, and Saul said to him,
"Blessed are you of the Lord! I have performed
the commandment of the Lord."

But Samuel said, "What then is this bleating of
the sheep in my ears, and the lowing of the oxen
which I hear?"

And Saul said, "They have brought them from the Amalekites; for the people spared the best of the sheep and the oxen, to sacrifice to the Lord your God; and the rest we have utterly destroyed."

Then Samuel said to Saul, "Be quiet! And I will tell you what the Lord said to me last night."

And he said to him, "Speak on."

So Samuel said, "When you were little in your own eyes, were you not head of the tribes of Israel? And did not the Lord anoint you king over Israel? Now the Lord sent you on a mission, and said, 'Go, and utterly destroy the sinners, the Amalekites, and fight against them until they are consumed.' Why then did you not obey the voice of the Lord? Why did you swoop down on the spoil, and do evil in the sight of the Lord?"

And Saul said to Samuel, "But I have obeyed the voice of the Lord, and gone on the mission on which the Lord sent me, and brought back Agag king of Amalek; I have utterly destroyed the Amalekites. But the people took of the plunder, sheep and oxen, the best of the things which should have been utterly destroyed, to sacrifice to the Lord your God in Gilgal."

So Samuel said:

"Has the Lord as great delight in burnt offerings and sacrifices,
As in obeying the voice of the Lord?
Behold, to obey is better than sacrifice,
And to heed than the fat of rams.
For rebellion is as the sin of witchcraft,
And stubbornness is as iniquity and idolatry.
Because you have rejected the word of the Lord,

He also has rejected you from being king."

Then Saul said to Samuel, "I have sinned, for I have transgressed the commandment of the Lord and your words, because I feared the people and obeyed their voice. Now therefore, please pardon my sin, and return with me, that I may worship the Lord."

But Samuel said to Saul, "I will not return with you, for you have rejected the word of the Lord, and the Lord has rejected you from being king over Israel."

And as Samuel turned around to go away, Saul seized the edge of his robe, and it tore. So Samuel said to him, "The Lord has torn the kingdom of Israel from you today, and has given it to a neighbor of yours, who is better than you. 29 And also the Strength of Israel will not lie nor relent. For He is not a man, that He should relent."

Then he said, "I have sinned; yet honor me now, please, before the elders of my people and before Israel, and return with me, that I may worship the Lord your God." So Samuel turned back after Saul, and Saul worshiped the Lord. (1 Samuel 15:1-31)

Here we have entered the middle of Saul's reign as the first king of Israel, which will end with him becoming a toxic leader. Saul was picked from the people and made king. The people chose Saul, but God anointed him. Speaking through Samuel the prophet, a burning issue God wanted addressed through Saul was a long standing generational problem. He wanted Saul to wipe out the Amalekites. They had deeply offended God by their history of being cruel and punishing towards Israel. God was ready to use King Saul to judge them. The time had come for God's purpose to be fulfilled in the life of Israel. So He raised up Saul to deal with it. His mission: kill everything that lived in Amalek.

Saul obeyed God...to a point. He went to battle with Amalek, like God said, but he didn't carry out the mission in its entirety. Instead of destroying every trace of that nation—"utterly destroy all that they have, and do not spare them"—he took the best for himself and allowed the people to do the same. One of the first things we learn about leaders that are unhealthy is that they have compromise in their lives. God has told them to do something, but they have only done it half way.

Saul's sin of compromise happened when he saved the good things, and tossed out the bad. His unwillingness to go all the way and "utterly destroy" Amalek, his willingness to listen to the voice of others over God, led to his compromising actions, which cost him his throne and anointing. It created a calamity that eventually claimed the life of his son. Remember, Saul was chosen. He was anointed. God had moved Samuel to bless him and place him as king over the nation. The prophet hoped things would go well. But it didn't, and Saul grieved God with his compromise.

LOST THROUGH DISOBEDIENCE

Time and time again, as I work with pastors and churches, I have seen this truth play out: authority releases hidden agendas. It's amazing how sweet someone can be until they get into a position of authority. This was true in Saul's life. He received authority and suddenly his character faults became tremendously apparent. These faults ultimately destroyed his destiny.

Before Saul became king, he was a man that shrunk back from attention. "And Saul the son of Kish was chosen. But when they sought him, he could not be found. Therefore they inquired of the Lord further, 'Has the man come here yet?' And the Lord answered, 'There he is, hidden among the equipment.' So they ran and brought him from there; and when he stood among the people, he was taller than any of the people from his shoulders upward." (1 Samuel 10:21-23) He was a humble man. He worked for his father. He followed through on what he was asked to do. Then, he became king. Overnight he gained prestige, fame, attention, approval, everything. He went into battles and won. He gained more and more fame. Then, God told him to fulfill his destiny and deliver his people from the hands of the Amalekites.

And he disobeyed God. One would think this was rock bottom for Saul. Wrong.

When Samuel confronted Saul, instead of sorrowfully repenting, he wanted to cover up his sin with a great church service and a big tithe check. He tried to repair through sacrifice what he destroyed through disobedience. God wouldn't have it. Samuel cursed him and told him that the call of God on his life had been withdrawn.

End of story, right? Nope. It got worse.

Saul remained king. He continued in the role without the anointing of God. He functioned on a platform of position, but had lost the grace to fulfill it. He is the portrait of what happens when compromise derails a leader who is unwilling to step aside. They use cover-ups to continue on despite the scandal and weakened power.

It is vital that we understand this: we cannot gain back through sacrifice what we've lost to disobedience. We can bring sacrifices to God, continue to worship Him, continue to serve Him, but because of our consistent disobedience, we can't repair through sacrifice what we have destroyed.

REBEL, WITCHCRAFT & SNARES

Samuel said that to rebel against God is the same as operating in witchcraft. They are equivalent in God's eyes. To be unwilling to bend our will to God's will is equivalent to idolatry because we are worshiping our will and not surrendering it to God. This is why God loves humility so much. It's a rare human commodity. Jesus prayed this hours before His death, "Father, if it is Your will, take this cup away from Me; nevertheless not My will, but Yours, be done." (Luke 22:42) Humility means we put His will above our own. Whenever He hears and sees someone walking in humility, it impresses God.

When God confronted Adam and Eve over their sin in the Garden, He began with Adam, the authority figure. In a home, when a father or mother do rebellious things against God, all kinds of destructive powers flood into that family. When we obey and surrender to God and the Lordship of Christ and the leading of the Holy Spirit, when we recognize authority and submit to Christ, we are protected with a shield around us. As Pastor Mark Batterson says, "When we violate our conscience by compromising our integrity, we put our reputation at risk. We also become our own advocate because we step outside the boundaries of God's good, pleasing, and perfect will. But when we obey God, we come under the umbrella of His protective authority. He is our Advocate. And it's His reputation that is at stake. If we don't give the Enemy a foothold, God won't let him touch a hair on our head."

Later in Saul's life, we see that a door opens to demonic oppression when we live in continual disobedience. People that are persistently disobedient in some part of their life, have opened a door to demons. In any kind of leadership role, whenever we rebel against God's order and Kingdom, whenever we leave the protection and grace of the Kingdom of God, we are subject and vulnerable to other spirits. When the Holy Spirit left Saul, a demonic power came over him.

I love people. I will pastor anybody that comes to my church. But I meet people that say they don't need a pastor, that church is crazy, that it's just them and Jesus. They are in rebellion. They are rejecting God's order. They are saying they don't need God's way. Nobody beats God's system. There's no plan B. He has the church, He has the family. We can't create a new form of family. We can't create a new order to replace the church.

Here's what made Saul the most unhealthy: he needed the approval of people. He could have repented but he didn't. He was not like David, who, when he was caught in murder and adultery, sincerely repented. But Saul didn't repent. When confronted, Saul asked Samuel to make things look good for him in front of the people. He was more concerned about what others thought than what God thought. When that is the condition of our lives, we are in trouble. Saul's concern was to pretend like it was all okay, when it definitely was not.

Leaders that need acceptance over anything else, will always end up losing the approval of God. When a leader uses the approval of people to meet their need for significance, they create an extremely harmful codependency. When we have authority or position or platform, there is a temporal reward of significance. We become important. The problem arises when we use people to meet our need instead of allowing God to meet our need. This will keep people under our leadership weak and immature as we need them to stay put and give us praise. We create a codependency when they can't do anything without a controlling leader's guidance or approval.

Whenever we think more about people's opinions of us more than what our integrity needs, we become unhealthy, unhappy and unusable to God.

And in Lystra a certain man without strength in his feet was sitting, a cripple from his mother's womb, who had never walked. 9 This man heard Paul speaking. Paul, observing him intently and seeing that he had faith to be healed, said with a loud voice, "Stand up straight on your feet!" And he leaped and walked. Now when the people saw what Paul had done, they raised their voices, saying in the Lycaonian language, "The gods have come down to us in the likeness of men!" And Barnabas they called Zeus, and Paul,

Hermes, because he was the chief speaker. Then the priest of Zeus, whose temple was in front of their city, brought oxen and garlands to the gates, intending to sacrifice with the multitudes.

But when the apostles Barnabas and Paul heard this, they tore their clothes and ran in among the multitude, crying out and saying, "Men, why are you doing these things? We also are men with the same nature as you, and preach to you that you should turn from these useless things to the living God, who made the heaven, the earth, the sea, and all things that are in them, who in bygone generations allowed all nations to walk in their own ways. Nevertheless He did not leave Himself without witness, in that He did good, gave us rain from heaven and fruitful seasons, filling our hearts with food and gladness." And with these sayings they could scarcely restrain the multitudes from sacrificing to them.

Then Jews from Antioch and Iconium came there; and having persuaded the multitudes, they stoned Paul and dragged him out of the city, supposing him to be dead. However, when the disciples gathered around him, he rose up and went into the city. And the next day he departed with Barnabas to Derbe. (Acts 14:8-20)

In the same day, Paul was worshiped as a god for healing a man and then stoned as a heretic. He didn't allow people's approval or disapproval to ruin his life, even after being stoned. If we live off of people's approval, it is just a matter of time until God will ween us from the oxygen of peoples acceptance. Why? "The fear of man brings a snare, But whoever trusts in the Lord shall be safe." (Proverbs 29:25) When God leads us to do something, we can't let what other people think of us cause us to stumble along the path.

THERE IS HOPE

It can be incredibly disorienting when a leader has become unhealthy. Many times, we take the brunt of their anger—like David did with Saul. We question and wonder why God would allow these things to happen. Samuel, the man that anointed Saul as king, was no different. His greatest disappointment was Saul's failure as King. He knew that Saul had such great potential to be a great and godly king, but he had completely squandered it. Samuel was deeply wounded by Saul's missed potential. He wasn't looking at things like God was—he needed God's perspective. God's will for His people cannot be forfeited by anyone's disobedience, including a leaders. God will remove leaders and put another in place who will obey Him.

> Now the Lord said to Samuel, "How long will you mourn for Saul, seeing I have rejected him from reigning over Israel? Fill your horn with oil, and go; I am sending you to Jesse the Bethlehemite. For I have provided Myself a king among his sons."
> And Samuel said, "How can I go? If Saul hears it, he will kill me."

But the Lord said, "Take a heifer with you, and say, 'I have come to sacrifice to the Lord.' 3 Then invite Jesse to the sacrifice, and I will show you what you shall do; you shall anoint for Me the one I name to you."

So it was, when they came, that he looked at Eliab and said, "Surely the Lord's anointed is before Him!"

But the Lord said to Samuel, "Do not look at his appearance or at his physical stature, because I have refused him. For the Lord does not see as man sees;[a] for man looks at the outward appearance, but the Lord looks at the heart."

And Samuel said to Jesse, "Are all the young men here?" Then he said, "There remains yet the youngest, and there he is, keeping the sheep."

And Samuel said to Jesse, "Send and bring him. For we will not sit down[b] till he comes here." 12 So he sent and brought him in. Now he was ruddy, with bright eyes, and good-looking. And the Lord said, "Arise, anoint him; for this is the one!" 13 Then Samuel took the horn of oil and anointed him in the midst of his brothers; and the Spirit of the Lord came upon David from that day forward. So Samuel arose and went to Ramah. (1 Samuel 16:1-3, 6-7, 11-13)

God was ready to move on with a new leader whether Samuel or anyone else was. He had things He wanted to do for his people. So, He raised up another person, David. He knew that David would do what the others were supposed to do. Nobody can change God's mind regarding what He has for us, for our cities, for our churches, for our families, and for this generation. He will wait until He finds someone that will believe him.

When Samuel anointed David as king, we learn another little lesson vital to being a leader: God anoints us early on for what He has assigned us to accomplish later in life. When we try to advance the season before the assignment is ready, we get frustrated. God knows the timing of His assignment. David waited over a decade for God to lead him into the full measure of his destiny. And when he did start to come into the measure, David defeated Goliath.

HOW DO WE SURVIVE?

We have looked at what causes leaders to get off track. We have seen how we can avoid going down the wrong trails ourselves and we have seen to how stay humble and healthy. What happens when a leader attacks us and tries to take us out? David stepped into his destiny and did what Saul was supposed to do. Saul was supposed to do what David did and he knew it. He grew angry. He couldn't bear to see the people giving David the attention he was supposed to get. He waged a war against the one that was to be his successor. An unhealthy leader wages war against gifted people that they think can take their place or their influence. Insecure leaders will drive away the very people God has sent them to mentor and raise up. So how do we survive a time when we are seen as threats instead of partners and heirs?

#1: Trust God for our life today and our destiny tomorrow.

When God is with us, we have to trust that no unhealthy leader has the power to destroy us. On three different occasions, Saul tried to kill David with a spear. Then a switch flipped and half an hour later he apologized. What kept David going through the brutal assassination attempts? He trusted that God would get him where he was supposed to be and when he was supposed to be there, even when he was under the influence of an unhealthy leader. He trusted that God would remove Saul from leadership when the time was right in His divine timing. It wasn't David's job to remove him.

And it isn't our job to remove unhealthy leaders either. Authority comes from God. "Let every soul be subject to the governing authorities. For there is no authority except from God, and the authorities that exist are appointed by God. Therefore whoever resists the authority resists the ordinance of God, and those who resist will bring judgment on themselves." (Romans 13:1-2) We have to respect the position, even when we don't respect the person. This is a condition of the heart and leads to the next point.

#2: Guard our hearts.

David eventually had to leave Saul's palace. On the run, God brought men to David that would eventually become his trusted men, army, and confidants. While fleeing from his life, David guarded his heart. Twice during the eleven year span he was on the run, David was in the position to kill Saul and didn't do it. One time is particularly notable:

Now it happened, when Saul had returned from following the Philistines, that it was told him, saying, "Take note! David is in the Wilderness of En Gedi." Then Saul took three thousand chosen men from all Israel, and went to seek David and his men on the Rocks of the Wild Goats. So he came to the sheepfolds by the road, where there was a cave; and Saul went in to attend to his needs. (David and his men were staying in the recesses of the cave.) Then the men of David said to him, "This is the day of which the Lord said to you, 'Behold, I will deliver your enemy into your hand, that you may do to him as it seems good to you.'" And David arose and secretly cut off a corner of Saul's robe. Now it happened afterward that David's heart troubled him because he had cut Saul's robe. And he said to his men, "The Lord forbid that I should do this thing to my master, the Lord's anointed, to stretch out my hand against him, seeing he is the anointed of the Lord." So David restrained his servants with these words, and did not allow them to rise against Saul. And Saul got up from the cave and went on his way.

David also arose afterward, went out of the cave, and called out to Saul, saying, "My lord the king!" And when Saul looked behind him, David stooped with his face to the earth, and bowed down. And David said to Saul: "Why do you listen to the words of men who say, 'Indeed David seeks your harm'? Look, this day your eyes have seen that the Lord delivered you today into my hand in the cave, and someone urged me to kill you. But my eye spared you, and I said, 'I will not stretch out my hand against my lord, for he is the Lord's anointed.' Moreover, my father, see! Yes, see the corner of your robe in my hand! For in that I cut off the corner of your robe, and did not kill you, know and see that there is neither evil nor rebellion in my hand, and I have not sinned against you. Yet you hunt my life to take it. Let the Lord judge between you and me, and let the Lord avenge me on you. But my hand shall not be against you. As the proverb of the ancients says, 'Wickedness proceeds from the wicked.' But my hand shall not be against you. After whom has the king of Israel come out? Whom do you pursue? A dead dog? A flea? Therefore let the Lord be judge, and judge between you and me, and see and plead my case, and deliver me out of your hand." (1 Samuel 24:1-15)

David didn't allow his heart to harden towards God and Saul to the point that he was willing to kill the man. The devil wants the opposite of us. The devil wants to make us bitter, hateful and vengeful. We can't let that happen. No matter how badly people have treated us, we can love and forgive them. Someone that acts like a monster can never turn us into monsters. David didn't; we don't have to either.

#3: **Pray for them.**
The enemy will tempt us to give a justification for bad behavior because someone has wronged us. Here is the answer to that: turn them over to Jesus in prayer. "Therefore I exhort first of all that supplications, prayers, intercessions, and giving of thanks be made for all

men, for kings and all who are in authority, that we may lead a quiet and peaceable life in all godliness and reverence. For this is good and acceptable in the sight of God our Savior, who desires all men to be saved and to come to the knowledge of the truth. For there is one God and one Mediator between God and men, the Man Christ Jesus, who gave Himself a ransom for all, to be testified in due time…" (1 Timothy 2:1-6) We are not called to criticize leaders. We are called to pray for them. When God sees us honoring authority and praying for them, God will give us the blessing someone in authority has kept from us. No one can steal from us what God wants delivered to us. We will find as we pray for leaders, God will give us love for them.

#4: Love them.

Jealousy, gossip and agendas are to be handled like Jesus would handle them. Through love.

> "You have heard that it was said, 'You shall love your neighbor and hate your enemy.' But I say to you, love your enemies, bless those who curse you, do good to those who hate you, and pray for those who spitefully use you and persecute you, that you may be sons of your Father in heaven; for He makes His sun rise on the evil and on the good, and sends rain on the just and on the unjust. For if you love those who love you, what reward have you? Do not even the tax collectors do the same? And if you greet your brethren only, what do you do more than others? Do not even the tax collectors do so? Therefore you shall be perfect, just as your Father in heaven is perfect." (Matthew 5:43-48)

Let's give God a chance to love those who have authority and who are unhealthy. We can distance ourselves from them but still love them. We can remove our lives from their authority and seek God's best for them. We can put a boundary between us and still honor their authority through love.

#5: Forgive them.

Saul knew in his spirit who David was called to be, but his soul was diseased. He could not release the blessing David needed. David was supposed to be like Saul's son, not his enemy. How many of us have been in relationships with unhealthy who wouldn't bless us and release us into God's calling for us? In each case, we have the chance to be more like Jesus and to grow through forgiving them. "For if you forgive men their trespasses, your heavenly Father will also forgive you. But if you do not forgive men their trespasses, neither will your Father forgive your trespasses." (Matthew 6:14-15)

#6: Don't wage war with them.

While Nehemiah was repairing the wall, outside the gate, his enemy was on the ground, yelling for him to come down to them. Nehemiah refused to leave his post. It's more important to follow Christ, to walk in love, and to live as a good disciple, than it is to descend down to someone else level and fight it out. Anybody can be angry, mean, hurtful, jealous. It takes someone willing to stick to their post, do their job, keep working, keep praying and keep loving, to see things done.

#7: Learn from their mistakes.

We have spent most of this chapter learning from

Saul's mistakes. Often, God will allow us to be in situations where we are exposed to toxic leaders. He will allow us to be a part of situations that at the moment are hard and tasking so we can learn what not to do when we are put into positions of authority. Once that season is over, He will show us how to put up a boundary and pray for them, love them and forgive them.

We should recognize our time with them was God teaching us through their mistakes. We want to learn from good and bad examples. That way we can intentionally direct our paths away from the mistakes others have made. Sometimes the best model for right behavior is the bad behavior of someone else.

#8: Don't let your life be shaped by other people.

If we don't conquer the seemingly insignificant areas in our lives God wants us to deal with, they will reign over us when we reach places of authority. One of those areas is in the realm of forgiveness. We will become like the person we refuse to love and forgive. Forgiveness and love gives us an escape mechanism from being polluted by others toxic acts.

#9: Worship God

Worshiping God keeps our hearts tender toward God and open to His Spirit filling us with love and forgiveness for those that are unhealthy around us. No matter the climate we are in, when we worship Jesus, we take a spiritual bath. He cleanses us and the atmosphere around us. David's best music came during his worst times. He worshiped his way through it all. We should work to make sure the devil can't take our worship. When we can worship God for being good when the devil is making things bad, we give him a black eye and we find health and deliverance flowing into all areas of our life.

CHAPTER FOUR
BREAKING THE POWER
OF UNGODLY SOUL TIES

*"You have soul ties with the people you sleep with and even
when you are no longer in bed with them, they remain in your
head. Your thoughts are consumed by their absence in your life.
We feel disconnected from something when we give away
our most prized bodily asset to a person that can't even spell
our last name correctly."*
*- Chris Marvel, Love Laws: Rules of Love and Relationship in
the 21st Century*

We are triune beings. We are a spirit, with a soul,
living in a body. "Now may the God of peace Himself
sanctify you completely; and may your whole spirit, soul,
and body be preserved blameless at the coming of our
Lord Jesus Christ." (1 Thessalonians 5:23). Everyone
who is alive has a spirit. Before we are saved, our spirit
is asleep, dead, or dormant. It resides in us, but it is not
functioning. When we are born again, our spirit comes
alive. It has to be regenerated through Christ and made
perfect. "…to the general assembly and church of the
firstborn who are registered in heaven, to God the Judge

of all, to the spirits of just men made perfect…" (Hebrews 12:23) The spirit is made perfect in God and we are "a new creation; old things have passed away; behold, all things have become new." (2 Corinthians 5:17) Our spirit also becomes the temple of the Holy Spirit. This means that our spirit is God's territory.

Our souls represent our personality. It is who we are. It is made up of our mind, will and emotions. That's where the action is: after our spirit is regenerated through Christ, our lifelong journey with Christ is to restore our souls by renewing our minds, repairing our emotions, and aligning our wills with God's kingdom. That is what God is doing in our journey together. The soul is rewired as we read, study and pray the Word. It is where we are transformed and renewed. And it is the primary place the devil wants to bind us up and destroy us with soul ties.

It is important to highlight here how stupid our flesh can be. God gains control over our flesh through the transformation of our souls and through the influence of our newborn spirit and its practices. If our flesh is in control of our lives, we won't do simple things like get out of bed, brush our teeth, comb our hair. We will be lazy and stay in bed. The flesh is governed by the soul. Romans 12 tells us to not be ruled by the world and its desires.

For this chapter, we will focus on the soul and how we can rid ourselves of one of the devil's strongest weapons in our lives: soul ties. To live the new life Christ died for, we have to change our souls. The fact that we believe people can change is a unique Christian thought. The concept in the world is that people can't change—once an addict, always an addict. That is not true in the kingdom of God. Jesus changes people. He does this first by restoring their souls.

> The Lord is my shepherd;
> I shall not want.
> He makes me to lie down in green pastures;
> He leads me beside the still waters.
> He restores my soul;
> He leads me in the paths of righteousness
> For His name's sake. (Psalms 23:1-3)

Our souls are damaged by the difficulties of life, through unhealthy relationships and by our sin. God is working, however, to reverse that and to restore our mind, our will and our emotions. Jesus is working with the Holy Spirit to restore it to its original design. This is vital to understand because some people have lost the power to make quality decisions. They can't stand up for anything because they have been so assaulted in their souls. They are unable to lay healthy boundaries. God wants that to change. "The law of the Lord is perfect, converting the soul; The testimony of the Lord is sure, making wise the simple…" (Psalm 19:7) The word "convert" in the Hebrew means "to be restored." The word of God restores our souls so we can live healthy lives.

HEALTHY SOUL TIES

What is a soul tie? It is the unseen linkage between two people in their soul. It can be very good. Before we dive into the unhealthy soul ties, let's look at the healthy ones.

It's God's will that we have healthy Biblical soul ties. One example is found in marriage. When Adam prophesied over Eve, he was speaking about God's plan for healthy soul ties:

> And Adam said:
> "This is now bone of my bones
> And flesh of my flesh;
> She shall be called Woman,
> Because she was taken out of Man."
> Therefore a man shall leave his father and mother and be joined to his wife, and they shall become one flesh. (Genesis 2:23-24)

All throughout the Bible, we are taught that man and woman become one flesh when they get married. The idea of one flesh is not just physical. Through physical intimacy, a bond in the soul occurs. We have a soul tie with people we sleep with. That is how God designed it. " And He answered and said to them, 'Have you not read that He who made them at the beginning "made them male and female," and said, "For this reason a man shall leave his father and mother and be joined to his wife, and the two shall become one flesh"? So then, they are no longer two but one flesh. Therefore what God has joined together, let not man separate.'" (Matthew 19:4-6)

Another example of a healthy soul tie is between parent and child. It is abnormal and destructive when a child and parent don't bond. Whenever a child grows up in an unloving environment, this adds all kinds of brokenness in lives that were already broken. The parent/child tie is supposed to be there. Parents reading this who have good ties with their children know what I am referring to. My kids are grown but they are still in my heart. I pray for my kids all the time because we are connected in a positive way.

A third healthy soul tie involves Godly friendships. 1 Samuel 18 tells us about David and Jonathan:

> Now when he had finished speaking to Saul, the soul of Jonathan was knit to the soul of David, and Jonathan loved him as his own soul. Saul took him that day, and would not let him go home to his father's house anymore. Then Jonathan and David made a covenant, because he loved him as his own soul. And Jonathan took off the robe that was on him and gave it to David, with his armor, even to his sword and his bow and his belt. (1 Samuel 18:1-4)

There is nothing strange about this, though some in the world would try to pervert the relationship they had. We all have met someone that we really connected with and they became our friend. Good and Godly friendships are greatly beneficial to our lives. Iron sharpens iron. Our lives become more healthy, the more healthy people we allow into it.

The body of Christ is the fourth example of a healthy soul tie. We are a family, not just people that get together once or twice a week in a building. We are children of God and He looks at us as his family. This is a key to grasp because of lot of people are distancing from others in church. We need to be vigilant for those who are wandering off from the body because we all play an important part in the body of Christ. Our differences make us better together.

THE ILL-ADVISED SEVERING
OF GODLY SOUL TIES

Before we dive deep into unhealthy soul ties, I want to touch on something many of us have never considered: the ill-advised severing of Godly soul ties. We live in a culture that promotes the cutting of off Godly relationships. If you don't believe me, look at the promotion of abortion by more than half our country. Abortion is the ultimate example of the severing of a Godly soul tie. It is not a new practice. It has been going on for thousands of years. It is a sign of a calloused generation who cares more about their own desires than they do health, Godly relationships.

Abortion was not practiced clinically as we know it today until more recent medical advancements. When a child in Old Testament times was unwanted, the parents or others would throw it into field.

> Again the word of the Lord came to me, saying, "Son of man, cause Jerusalem to know her abominations, and say, 'Thus says the Lord God to Jerusalem: "Your birth and your nativity are from the land of Canaan; your father was an Amorite and your mother a Hittite. As for your nativity, on the day you were born your navel cord was not cut, nor were you washed in water to cleanse you; you were not rubbed with salt nor wrapped in swaddling cloths. No eye pitied you, to do any of these things for you, to have compassion on you; but you were thrown out into the open field, when you yourself were loathed on the day you were born.

"And when I passed by you and saw you struggling in your own blood, I said to you in your blood, 'Live!' Yes, I said to you in your blood, 'Live!' I made you thrive like a plant in the field; and you grew, matured, and became very beautiful. Your breasts were formed, your hair grew, but you were naked and bare. (Ezekiel 16:1-7)

The discarded child would lie in the field with the umbilical cord, and the blood of the mother still covering it; what a startling image. There are two things I want to point out here: first, the physical act of aborting children is barbaric and ungodly. It is murder and should be seen as so. Secondly, the act of abortion is a symbolic thing many people do to others. God spoke to me many are suffering in life because they have been discarded by others. When people are discarded by others, if the cord is not cut, they won't know true life. When peoples lives haven't been cut from unhealthy relationships and bonds with others, their life becomes diseased. They end up needy and hurt by it.

I want to tell those out there that were dumped in a field (spiritually, relationally, mentally, emotionally), who were uncared for, who were left for dead, that you are to LIVE! God says LIVE! It doesn't matter who broke your heart. It doesn't matter how many cords or ties are wrapped around you. The word of God has come down and it says that you are going to LIVE.

God has come to remove every curse and tie that is trying to destroy our lives. He desires that every unhealthy soul tie be cut off.

UNHEALTHY SOUL TIES

It is God's will for us to recognize, repent, and remove the influence of ungodly soul ties. It is God's will for no one else to interfere with His governing influence. No influence outside of God should have a disproportionate place of power and decision making in our lives. To break unhealthy soul ties, we need to recognize how they entered our lives in the first place.

1. Sexual intimacy outside of marriage.

> Do you not know that your bodies are members of Christ? Shall I then take the members of Christ and make them members of a harlot? Certainly not! Or do you not know that he who is joined to a harlot is one body with her? For "the two," He says, "shall become one flesh." But he who is joined to the Lord is one spirit with Him.
>
> Flee sexual immorality. Every sin that a man does is outside the body, but he who commits sexual immorality sins against his own body. Or do you not know that your body is the temple of the Holy Spirit who is in you, whom you have from God, and you are not your own? For you were bought at a price; therefore glorify God in your body and in your spirit, which are God's. (1 Corinthians 6:15-20)

By the Holy Spirit, we are literally united with Christ. He is the head, we are the body. Harlotry, in the Bible does not mean guys can do anything they desire and women can only sleep with one man or they are a harlot. Sexual immorality hurts everyone. Sex is not limited to the physical function. It is a spiritual act as well. It is the only thing that we do besides worship that engages spirit, soul and body. When we are intimate with a person, our souls join. That was established by God to develop closeness and bonds in marriage. Outside of marriage, it has tremendous negative consequences.

Flee sexual immorality. Paul says, in the New Testament, to fight the devil, bind him, cast him out. Don't give in to the devil. But when sexual sin shows up, he says we should flee. He writes this so we don't put ourselves in a place to fall. I've had a lot of young couples who are dating tell me that they were going to get together and read their Bibles and pray, with no one else home. I tell them I know that is their intention, but maybe they should flee that situation.

Flee sexual temptation. Why? Sexual sin is a sin against our souls. We need to teach people that are hooking up before they even date, let alone marry, that this is detrimental to their souls, and psychological health. We want to return to the sanctity and sacredness of sex. Sex is God's plan and it's great in marriage. Marriage for sex, sex for marriage.

Our bodies are temples of the Holy Spirit. The Bible says that God's Spirit lives in us. Gnosticism, in the time of Paul, taught that the most important thing for a man is his thoughts , feelings, and emotions about and towards God. The body was secondary. It didn't matter as much what they did with the body in regards to worshiping God. They could do anything with their body as long as they kept their mind on God. We have to reclaim the truth that what we do with our bodies impacts our spirit and soul as well as our body. We are triune beings. We can't separate the three into different parts and not have them influence one another. The most destructive way a soul tie forms a grip on a soul is from sex outside of marriage.

There's more to sex than mere skin on skin. Sex is as much spiritual mystery as physical fact. As written in Scripture, "The two become one." Since we want to become spiritually one with the Master, we must not pursue the kind of sex that avoids commitment and intimacy, leaving us more lonely than ever—the kind of sex that can never "become one." There is a sense in which sexual sins are different from all others. In sexual sin we violate the sacredness of our own bodies, these bodies that were made for God-given and God-modeled love, for "becoming one" with another. Or didn't you realize that your body is a sacred place, the place of the Holy Spirit? Don't you see that you can't live however you please, squandering what God paid such a high price for? The physical part of you is not some piece of property belonging to the spiritual part of you. God owns the whole works. So let people see God in and through your body. (1 Corinthians 6:15-20: The Message)

There is a masculine personality to most of Proverbs because they were written by a father for his son. Solomon mentions four or five times in his Proverbs that sex is fiery and can destroy us when it is outside of God's design. Sex is explosive.

Here is what we know from science. A biologist, in the 1980's, discovered that when we have sex with someone, we are having sex with everyone they have ever had sex with in their past. When two people try to get close, they don't understand that they have brought to the relationship all the people from their past. People experience mental oppression, and all kinds of anxiety, and they keep going from one sick relationship to another, it is often due to the fact that they have a soul tie that has perverted or distorted their views of life.

What we want to do is bring as few people to our marriage as possible. It's hard enough being married to one person. The devil oppresses us through the people that we were intimate with before marriage. Even if we are saved, and have married the one that God has called us to marry, issues from our past will pop up. Maybe it is that we can't stop thinking about an old partner. Maybe we are tormented by dreams of them in our lives. Maybe we have a soul tie that has to be broken off of us.

2. Close friendships with toxic people.

> Do not be deceived: "Evil company corrupts good habits."
> (1 Corinthians 15:33)

> Make no friendship with an angry man,
> And with a furious man do not go,
> Lest you learn his ways
> And set a snare for your soul.
> (Proverbs 22:24, 25)

What happens in an unbalanced friendship and relationship? We are pulled into behaviors we don't choose. We inherit them by being around that person. We have to guard the inner circle of our lives. We need to make sure we are not allowing toxic people into close proximity of our lives. We need to know when a relationship has become unbalanced and unhealthy. When their input is causing us to behave in ways that we wouldn't have before they came into our lives.

If someone is a recovering drug addict or alcoholic, they need to keep those friends out of their life that still drink and dope up. If someone is married and slept around before marriage and they have friends that still play the field, they need to cut those friends loose so they don't end up cheating on their spouse.

3. Family relationships.
This falls into two categories: over-involved parents or no parental tie at all.

One of the problems I see a lot, as a pastor, is parental interference in a new marriage. Often, one of the parents will have a problem stepping back after their child gets married. Parents must allow their kids to create their own family without influencing them. Married couples have to make decisions between themselves that does not include the mother-in-law or father-in-law.

The strongest bond in the universe is between mother and child. When bonds that are supposed to be healthy instruments are broken, there is a consequence. When we don't bond with one, or both of our parents, there is always an effect.

This is so vital. We have a broken hearted generation. They don't have physically or emotionally present fathers. When that bond is missing, people go searching for that need to be filled. Sometimes they are searching in the wrong place. Jesus knows how to heal us so powerfully, that any kind of cord that is attached to family pain can and will be broken. One reason God kept working with Abraham was that he saw Abraham was discipling everyone in his family sphere. He was working to make sure that their souls were shaped properly. Abraham was fathering before he was a father. This is what this generation needs and what only God can fill if it has been broken.

SYMPTOMS OF SOUL TIES

Discovering if we have soul ties is easy once we know the symptoms, so here are a few of them:

1. Irrational thinking, loss of mental clarity, and loss of reason.
Sometimes we need more than another cup of coffee to focus. Sometimes we need to get the junk out of our heads. We need deliverance from imposing negative thoughts in our lives.

2. Obsessive preoccupation with another person.
This doesn't have to be because of sex, but it often comes because sexual intercourse has taken place. This can also be seen when someone keeps going back to a person for acceptance, even when that person keeps abusing them. A soul tie is keeping them bound together.

3. Mood shifts based on a person's absence or presence.

4. Thinking about someone constantly.
Any person that we spend a lot of time with, we will develop a bond with. Men and women, we have to be

careful with the people we work with and associate with. Almost every affair doesn't begin as a physical thing. It started as a "time" thing. Two people spent too much time together and they formed a bond. Then it seemed like a natural expression to become intimate. They let a boundary be crossed. I have purposely set up severe boundaries with women. I don't counsel women alone in my office. In my life I don't go into the office alone. My wife is always with me when I'm there. We have to protect ourselves and put boundaries up.

5. Inability to make a decision without someone's approval or input.

Whenever someone's influence has weakened our will and we feel like we can't trust our own decision making without their input, we have a soul tie.

6. Inability to stop seeing or having sex with someone they know isn't good for them.

Wonderful people can have their lives devastated from a relationship they entered into innocently, lovingly, hopefully, never knowing where it was going. They didn't realize the hell that was awaiting them and are desperate to get out the tumultuous relationship.

7. Stalking someone on social media.

We shouldn't use social media to see if we can find someone from twenty years ago like an old flame in order to stir up the old romance or passion.

8. A willingness to do ANYTHING to make the relationship work.

This includes sacrificing moral boundaries. It's not healthy to sell our soul to keep someone in a relationship.

Anybody that makes us violate our conscience is not a friend or love interest.

9. Staying with that person even when relationship is toxic.

I'm not one for divorce, but the Bible does give us the right to divorce when it comes to adultery or abuse (verbal and physical). If someone is getting beaten, it is time to get out.

10. Memories from the past keep playing over and over again.

The devil has no right to dominate our memories or dream life with painful memories from our past. Even if dramatic things took place, by the blood of Jesus, we can be set free and sanctified from those things.

11. Unexplainable demonic oppression in our souls.

We have no idea what is at play in peoples families. If we enter into an intimate relationship with someone whose family members are in the occult, those spirits have a door into our lives. I have seen the most wonderful people have seasons of demonic oppression that are unthinkable, usually because of a soul tie that hasn't been broken.

12. An inability to establish and maintain healthy relationships.

A pattern of failing at relationships or always sabotaging healthy relationships, is often because there is an unhealthy connection. We need healthy relationships to live healthy lives.

GETTING FREE & STAYING FREE

The Holy Spirit is so powerful that He can set us free from the soul ties in our lives. If we have tied ourselves to someone, God can set us free and begin His work of helping us live free.

First, we have to know that anything in our lives that we recognize, repent or renounce can be broken and healed. If any unhealthy soul tie—intimacy, family, friends—is in your life now is the time to break it. Pray with me:

> "Lord I repent for allowing this tie to assume a controlling influence in my life. Thank you for forgiving me. Thank you for helping me. I recognize it's there. I bring it to you. I confess my fault to you. I admit it and I believe that you are ridding my life of it. In the Mighty Name of Jesus, I declare I am God's child. I have been washed in the blood of Jesus. I belong to God. Jesus is my Lord and Savior. The Holy Spirit lives in me. In the name of Jesus, I renounce and I rebuke and I break every soul tie in my life that's not healthy. Thank you for cutting those cords now. I am free in Christ. Amen."

After we repent or renounce those things, we have to surrender the self to Christ on a daily basis. We must begin to walk free of the ties by turning our lives over to Him anew everyday. Allowing Him to fill us with His love and acceptance, allowing the Holy Spirit to guide us into the right relationships, is the only way to stay free.

Submission to Christ makes taking a stand against Satan possible. When the devil comes back and tries to tie us up again, rebuke him.

And as we submit and take a stand, we can set the boundary. This is often easier said than done—especially when it comes to family soul ties. But we have to have boundaries to live healthy. One easy way to do this is to follow Paul's admonition: "Do not be unequally yoked together with unbelievers. For what fellowship has righteousness with lawlessness? And what communion has light with darkness?" (2 Corinthians 6:14)

By using this as a boundary, we will avoid heartache in our business. We won't tie ourselves to people that don't have the same beliefs and avoid a lot of pain in business. We won't develop bonds with friends that aren't walking with Christ, with those that are combative with our faith. Walking with Jesus is hard enough without having a close-knit friend trying to steer us away from Jesus. And this will keep us out of other people's beds that aren't (1) believers and (2) our future spouses. We should never commit to a relationship before they committed themselves to Christ Jesus as their Lord.

CHAPTER FIVE
OVERCOMING DELILAH

Pleasure without God, without the sacred boundaries, will actually leave you emptier than before. And this is biblical truth, this is experiential truth. The loneliest people in the world are amongst the wealthiest and most famous who found no boundaries within which to live. That is a fact I've seen again and again.
- Ravi Zacharias

Let me be very plain: pornography is not a joke. It is destructive and demonic. This evil polluting our land must be dealt with. This sin has invaded all areas of life—the church!—and has found it's way into the youngest of minds—eleven year old boys. If our future generation is to have healthy sexual lives, we must help them. We must deal with the spirit of immorality embodied in pornography. To do that, we will look at the story of Samson and Delilah and discover how we break her influence and set up healthy, sexual boundaries to keep this spirit out of our lives and the lives of those we love.

WE NEED SEXUAL BOUNDARIES

This generation is morally and psychologically unsafe. I am determined to help the generations after me become free from the trap of immorality, which has it starts with pornography. Pornography is an epidemic in this generation. We have to get to work in the body of Christ to free the future generations of boys and girls from this wicked thing. Here are some stats:

- 11 years old is the average age of first introduction
- By the time children are 14, 98% have watched pornography or been exposed to it
- Many young boys are becoming addicted by the age of 14
- 70% of men watch or view pornography
- 30% of women watch or view pornography
- Millennials, at a rate of 98%, think that porn is benign and that it doesn't hurt. Why? They are overexposed and desensitized to it.

That is just a small sampling of the findings regarding the proliferation of porn. It is wide spread and it is available and free. It is on our computers, on our TVs, on our phones. It is everywhere and it is being praised by the culture that it is shaping. But what is it really doing to the brains of those watching it?

Psychology used to commonly think that addictions were related solely to chemical based things like alcohol, drugs or cigarettes. But now we know that people can be addicted to behaviors like gambling or sex or other activities. Specifically, scientists have found that pornography changes the way the brain works and is as addictive as cocaine.

Our brains have a pleasure center. It's a powerful reward component designed to make us feel good when doing certain things so we will keep doing them. For example if you work out, do Crossfit or Yoga, that activity releases chemicals in the brain that make it rewarding. We might be in pain in our bodies, but our brain tells us that we did a good thing. When we eat good food, the things that taste good trigger a release of chemicals in the pleasure center. Why? We are supposed to eat and we are supposed to exercise.

God made the brain to want things that are good. This wanting comes from the pleasure center. When we have sex, God allows our brain to release a reward chemical because we are supposed to be sexual. Dopamine, the reward chemical, is released in the pleasure center and we learn very quickly that sex is good.

Pornography is a counterfeit to sex, but our brains don't know the difference. It just knows that dopamine is rushing in, and that means good things are happening. As the brain experiences the advanced, immediate and extreme high of pornography, it impacts the pleasure and reward center. Pornography, like other physically stimulating things, tricks the brain to keep wanting more and more. It becomes a high priority. People begin to crave the repetition.

Scientists have seen that during the act of watching porn, there is an over stimulation in the brain. To cope with the over-release of dopamine, the brain sets about undoing some of the pleasure receptors in the wiring. This is the only way that it can handle the flood that is coming in. The more porn is viewed, the more pleasure receptors are killed off. This means, over time, it takes more and more porn to have the same high that was once experienced. Porn users become desensitized due to the overwhelming flood of dopamine—the chemical used to tell us that something is a good action. They feed their mind so much, that dopamine floods the system and the receptors go offline.

To bolster what I am saying, scientists have found that pornography is as addictive as cocaine. It touches the pleasure center and awakens rewards in much the same way that cocaine does. Often, when a person is breaking free from porn, they become anxious and nervous, as one does in detoxing from an addictive drug such as cocaine. Their brains have become like an addicts brain. They have become used to the dopamine because pornography is also adept at forming long lasting pathways in the brain. No other human activity that people do can stand up against the onslaught of porn.

I say all of that to say this: Jesus Christ wants our men and sons and daughters and women free of porn. The church and His people can't change the world when their souls are bound to pornography.

THE SPIRIT OF IMMORALITY

In the Old Testament, we see two men who had supernatural capacities and both men forfeited their supernatural gifts for immorality. One of them was Solomon, gifted with wisdom. The other one was Samson with his gift of strength. The smartest man that ever lived lost his heritage and status in heaven and earth because he had thousands of wives and mistresses. The strongest man that ever lived would not commit to women, but slept with harlots and lost his strength. This ancient spirit has been at work for a very long time. By looking into Samson's story, we can see how to get free from the immoral spirit loosed through pornography. God gives us a great illustration of the seductive, sexually immoral spirit we see running rampant in our culture in the story of Samson and Delilah.

We find that early in Samson's life, he fell in love and he married a woman. However, before their marriage was consummated, his wife was murdered. Samson was the victim of a horrific life trauma. Due to this trauma, Samson found it difficult to re-engage relationally. Being a healthy man meant he still had sexual needs. He began having sex with multiple partners without developing loving relationships.

> Now Samson went to Gaza and saw a harlot there, and went in to her. When the Gazites were told, "Samson has come here!" they surrounded the place and lay in wait for him all night at the gate of the city. They were quiet all night, saying, "In the morning, when it is daylight, we will kill him." And Samson lay low till midnight; then he arose at midnight, took hold of the doors of the gate of the city and the two gateposts, pulled them up, bar and all, put them on his shoulders, and carried them to the top of the hill that faces Hebron. (Judges 16:1-3)

We see Samson's gift of strength on display here. Through an angelic visitation when he was young and the fact that he kept some of the Nazarite vow he had made, God gave him the gift of supernatural strength. He carried off the city gates, something he couldn't have done naturally. But his prolonged engagement in an immoral lifestyle was starting to take a toll. What started as merely meeting a need, finally took over his life. His emotions become engaged in his actions. He couldn't stop himself. He began having sex with Delilah and things were never the same.

"Afterward it happened that he loved a woman in the Valley of Sorek, whose name was Delilah." (Judges 16:4) Her name means "to bring down by languishing; to bring something low." His sexual relations with Delilah took hold of his life, and he fell in love with her. Things escalated from there:

> And the lords of the Philistines came up to her and said to her, "Entice him, and find out where his great strength lies, and by what means we may overpower him, that we may bind him to afflict him; and every one of us will give you eleven hundred pieces of silver."
>
> So Delilah said to Samson, "Please tell me where your great strength lies, and with what you may be bound to afflict you."
>
> And Samson said to her, "If they bind me with seven fresh bowstrings, not yet dried, then I shall become weak, and be like any other man."
>
> So the lords of the Philistines brought up to her seven fresh bowstrings, not yet dried, and she bound him with them. Now men were lying in wait, staying with her in the room. And she said to him, "The Philistines are upon you, Samson!" But he broke the bowstrings as a strand of yarn breaks when it touches fire. So the secret of his strength was not known.

Then Delilah said to Samson, "Look, you have mocked me and told me lies. Now, please tell me what you may be bound with."

So he said to her, "If they bind me securely with new ropes that have never been used, then I shall become weak, and be like any other man."

Therefore Delilah took new ropes and bound him with them, and said to him, "The Philistines are upon you, Samson!" And men were lying in wait, staying in the room. But he broke them off his arms like a thread.

Delilah said to Samson, "Until now you have mocked me and told me lies. Tell me what you may be bound with."

And he said to her, "If you weave the seven locks of my head into the web of the loom"—

So she wove it tightly with the batten of the loom, and said to him, "The Philistines are upon you, Samson!" But he awoke from his sleep, and pulled out the batten and the web from the loom.

Then she said to him, "How can you say, 'I love you,' when your heart is not with me? You have mocked me these three times, and have not told me where your great strength lies." And it came to pass, when she pestered him daily with her words and pressed him, so that his soul was vexed to death, that he told her all his heart, and said to her, "No razor has ever come upon my head, for I have been a Nazirite to God from my mother's womb. If I am shaven, then my strength will leave me, and I shall become weak, and be like any other man."

When Delilah saw that he had told her all his heart, she sent and called for the lords of the Philistines, saying, "Come up once more, for he has told me all his heart." So the lords of the Philistines came up to her and brought the money in their hand. Then she lulled him to sleep on her knees, and called for a man and had him shave off the seven locks of his head. Then she began to torment him,[a] and his strength left him. And she said, "The Philistines are upon you, Samson!" So he awoke from his sleep, and said, "I will go out as before, at other times, and shake myself free!" (Judges 16:5-20)

Delilah, in the context of this teaching, represents a spirit of immorality and sexual temptation. In the book of Judges she is a woman, but that doesn't mean that immorality is tied only to women. Immorality affects both sexes. I am addressing sexual temptation and the six things that Delilah/sexual temptation did to Samson, so we can glean understanding from this story:

1. She enticed him.

Enticement comes when a desire is discovered and the desire offers fulfillment. She tempted him with the thing he wanted. Pornography and sexual temptation draws us with something every human being wants: sexual satisfaction.

2. She pestered him daily with her words.

Whenever we are struggling with immorality, there is an internal narrative in our soul. There is a continual battering ram of condemnation and shame coming from the sin. It will wear us down if we don't run to God, repent and ask for help.

3. She pressed him.

The temptation didn't let up because Samson kept going back for more.

4. He felt vexed.

There was still hope for him at this point. He could still feel the Holy Spirit's conviction. He could have escaped at this point. God is so merciful. When people are engaged in a sinful season of life, God will keep trying to pull them back. His mercy endures forever. Judgment is always the last stop to changing our lives. Samson shaking off the new bonds Delilah tied him with was a sign of God's mercy in Samson's life. He was allowing Samson to see the trap she was laying out for him in hopes Samson would turn his life around. But he didn't. Notice there is almost always no immediate consequence to the sins we chronically commit. Everything seems great for a while. A train will fly down the rails at the same speed it was going when the engine was running. People who do not address the immorality in their life are like that train with the engine turned off. They just don't know it yet. At some point, the train will come to a stuttering halt and all hell will break loose.

5. She lulled him to sleep.

If we aren't careful, we will allow chronic sins to dull our senses. We will fall asleep to it's impact on our life. One of the things that habitual sin—specifically, sexual sin—does is to lull us to slumber. We stop feeling convicted about doing wrong. We should love it when God makes us feel bad about our sins. It is a sign that God's love is still active in our lives. The conviction of the Holy Spirit means He's protecting us.

6. She tormented him.

We see in Samson's this truth: what we give in to will belittle and torment our very existence. Why? Because we have betrayed God and His designs for our lives.

THE RESULTS OF NO SEXUAL BOUNDARIES

Once the sexual immorality in his life had fully consumed him and he was tormented by it, he was taken captive. "...he did not know that the Lord had departed from him. Then the Philistines took him..." (Judges 16:21) When the Philistines got hold of Samson, the first thing he lost was his vision, which to us represents prophetic vision. "...and put out his eyes..."

Then they "brought him down to Gaza." (Judges 16:21) This was not a place he wanted to be. He was surrounded by his enemies. He became depressed. Whenever we lose sight of God's calling in our lives depression walks in. When hope walks out, depression walks in. God wants us to believe that our tomorrow is going to be better than our today. God wants us to believe the best is yet to come. When we stop believing in the future God has for us, something blinds us to the prophetic future God has for us. Now, sometimes, that is discouragement, but other times, its a chronic sin that we haven't dealt with.

Once he was depressed, "...[t]hey bound him with bronze fetters, and he became a grinder in the prison." (Judges 16: 21) Early on, Samson could have broken those chains like they were little kids toys. But his strength was gone. He was bound. It's interesting to note, there was a long period of time when he was being immoral, and he was still free to function. At some point, the immorality took over and he became bound. If we flirt with something long enough, it will tie us up, enslave us, and imprison us.

Life became a grind for him. Life became passionless, hopeless and visionless for Samson. He was defeated and walked in a circle like an animal. Our lives are not supposed to be an endless grind. It's supposed to be a daily adventure with Jesus Christ. He has so many great stories for our lives to tell. That's what our journey with Christ is supposed to be—a great adventure! But when we fall so deep into sexual immorality, nothing stays alive for us. Life becomes a grind as we now serve the thing that once pleased us so much.

If we don't turn back to God and ask for forgiveness and help from Him, we will find that we have lost our vision for life. We will become depressed as the sin drags us deeper into bondage. We will be bound and life will become a grind. But it doesn't have to be that way. We can find freedom from pornography's grip and from sexual temptation's snares.

MARRIAGE: THE BOUNDARY
FOR BIBLICALLY-BASED SEXUAL LIVES

God gives us sexual boundaries not because He's an uptight old man in the sky. He does it because He knows what's best for us. He's a father to His children. The Bible is the "how to manual" for our lives. The things that God says aren't old fashion rules. They are eternal principles that will make or break our lives if we keep or violate them.

God is not against sex. We don't have to live in fear of sex. In case you hadn't noticed, the God that created the heavens, the earth, everything, made men and women and He made us sexual beings. Sex, as God created, was not meant to be just about procreation. It is also pleasure-filled. He built that into the act. Sex is for the intimate relationship in marriage. Sex helps keep a couple close their entire lives.

> It's good for a man to have a wife, and for a woman to have a husband. Sexual drives are strong, but marriage is strong enough to contain them and provide for a balanced and fulfilling sexual life in a world of sexual disorder. The marriage bed must be a place of mutuality—the husband seeking to satisfy his wife, the wife seeking to satisfy her husband. Marriage is not a place to "stand up for your rights." Marriage is a decision to serve the other, whether in bed or out. Abstaining from sex is permissible for a period of time if you both agree to it, and if it's for the purposes of prayer and fasting—but only for such times. Then come back together again. Satan has an ingenious way of tempting us when we least expect it. I'm not, understand, commanding these periods of abstinence—only providing my best counsel if you should choose them. (1 Corinthians 7:2-6; The Message)

This bears repeating: God is not against sex. He invented it. He wants us to enjoy it in marriage. The marriage bed must be a place of mutual enjoyment. It is the place where the husband seeks to please his wife and the wife to please her husband. The marriage bed is not the place to stand up for your rights. The marriage bed is the place to serve the other person.

> Drink water from your own cistern,
> And running water from your own well.
> Should your fountains be dispersed abroad,
> Streams of water in the streets?
> Let them be only your own,
> And not for strangers with you.
> Let your fountain be blessed,
> And rejoice with the wife of your youth.
> As a loving deer and a graceful doe,
> Let her breasts satisfy you at all times;
> And always be enraptured with her love.
> For why should you, my son, be enraptured by an immoral woman,
> And be embraced in the arms of a seductress?
> (Proverbs 5:15-20)

Do you know the saying, "Drink from your own rain barrel, draw water from your own spring-fed well"?

It's true. Otherwise, you may one day come home and find your barrel empty and your well polluted.

Your spring water is for you and you only, not to be passed around among strangers.

Bless your fresh-flowing fountain!

Enjoy the wife you married as a young man!

Lovely as an angel, beautiful as a rose—don't

ever quit taking delight in her body. Never take her love for granted!

Why would you trade enduring intimacies for cheap thrills with a whore? for dalliance with a promiscuous stranger? (Proverbs 5:15-20; The Message)

The Bible gives us these directions, these guidelines, these boundaries to keep sex in marriage. It is to be a place of passion, satisfaction, continuity and faithfulness.

GETTING & STAYING FREE

Jesus Christ can restore your sexual purity and innocence. Jesus Christ can deliver you from any form of sexual bondage or addiction. Jesus Christ can heal your life from all your trauma and pain of past sexual experiences. Jesus Christ can set you free from porn. Jesus Christ can remove and replace all your pain and shame with His love.

Our brain is made up of billions of nerves called neurons. They carry trillions of signals. Our brains are making more phone calls right now than every phone on the planet. Our brain is an amazing, fearfully made, wonder. The brain uses 20% of our body's energy and oxygen. It devours resources. Brain pathways compete for functioning power. The unused pathways are replaced. Anything you don't use, you lose. Anything you stop using in your mind, it goes away. This is so key to getting free from sexual and pornography addiction.

We know that our minds change our brains. The thoughts that we have remap the brain. We call this neural plasticity: the brain can change. When we change our thoughts, we literally change the construction of the brain. God has given the brain the incredible potential to change. "And do not be conformed to this world, but be transformed by the renewing of your mind, that you may prove what is that good and acceptable and perfect will of God." (Romans 12:2) Any area of your life can change, and it starts in the brain.

In cognitive behavioral counseling, we use new, Godly thoughts to short circuit therapy. When we put new, Godly thoughts into the brain, they will overtake the way that we think about life. Neurological pathways in our minds—the human thought superhighways—can be shut down, covered, destroyed. Yes, when a person views porn, it tricks the brain into thinking that it is a healthy experience. Yes, that creates a powerful brain pathway that can stay with people. But that can be changed, despite what the modern day, humanistic society says. It is simple, yet hard. To stop it, we have do the opposite of what we are currently doing and we have to begin undoing things by introducing new thoughts—God's thoughts.

I want to reiterate, that when porn pathways in the brain are not used, they will disappear and be replaced with something else. God can help people retrain their brain about sex.

The Bible is so powerful, it is unlike any other book or words. When the Word enters our mind, there is nothing it can't conquer and change. When you feed the mind the Word of God, it can overcome negative, destructive neural pathways and change the habitual thinking patterns that are wrong. Our mind can change. What are some of God's thoughts that can help us start the process of being free?

> "I have made a covenant with my eyes;
> Why then should I look upon a young woman?"
> (Job 31:1)

> I will set nothing wicked before my eyes;
> I hate the work of those who fall away;
> It shall not cling to me. (Psalm 101:3)

In adding to the verses above, we can take a few minutes and go over the simple steps listed below. They are easy to follow and can help us start the process of finding freedom and building boundaries around our lives concerning sexual matters:

1. Repent and allow Jesus to love on us.

When we humble ourselves, admit we have made mistakes, and then worship Jesus through His word, through prayer, through song, we will His presence enveloping us. We will find healing for our hearts and strength to fight the temptations that come our way.

2. Put the word of God into our brain and allow it to reshape how we think.

God can rewire our brain through His Word. All the ungodly sexual experiences fall away. The grip of porn on our life will disappear. It will be as if it never happened in the brain.

3. Become accountable to others.

Men are under assault. They need accountability. They need resources so that they can get help and stay away from this trap. This can begin in your church, in your circle of close friends, and through other local and national ministries that help men find help.

4. Receive the restored innocence that you once had.

Two women that followed Christ had been prostitutes. One of them had seven demons. They became holy women of God. Their innocence was restored by the love of Christ.

5. Work with the Holy Spirit to stay away from things that will snare us.

The Holy Spirit can deliver anyone from anything. Be sensitive to His warnings and do not allow compromise.

6. Keep the freedom by renewing the mind through reading and memorizing the word.

Keeping the pathways of your brain filled with the Word of God is vital to replacing the old ways of thinking and overcoming the images that will come into our minds.

CHAPTER SIX
CONTENTMENT

Revenge, lust, ambition, pride, and self-will are too often exalted as the gods of man's idolatry; while holiness, peace, contentment, and humility are viewed as unworthy of a serious thought.
- Charles Spurgeon

Contentment is the only real wealth.
- Alfred Nobel

True contentment is a thing as active as agriculture.
It is the power of getting out of any situation all that there is in it.
It is arduous and it is rare.
- Gilbert K. Chesterton

Esau ran to meet him, and embraced him, and fell on his neck and kissed him, and they wept. And he lifted his eyes and saw the women and children, and said, "Who are these with you?"

So he said, "The children whom God has graciously given your servant." Then the maidservants came near, they and their children, and bowed down. And Leah also came near with her children, and they bowed down. Afterward Joseph and Rachel came near, and they bowed down.

Then Esau said, "What do you mean by all this company which I met?"

And he said, "These are to find favor in the sight of my lord."

But Esau said, "I have enough, my brother; keep what you have for yourself." (Genesis 33:4-9)

Jacob and Esau met after a lifetime of massive conflict and struggle. They had reached an age of maturity and, in their greeting, there is a revelation that Esau had found contentment in life. He had enough to be satisfied. He was content in what God had given him and the fight Jacob expected didn't occur. What I have realized in my life, is that people who don't need things, people who are content in life, can change the world. These are people that are not looking for personal advantage; it seems they have an easier time doing things for Jesus. They are fully satisfied by Jesus and can get things done for Him.

Imagine a life where the prayer of the heart is: "God, it is enough, I have you!" What would the world be like if our happiness wasn't based on whether we have something we want or whether we are doing the things we want? What if our happiness was based not on cars, homes or spouses, but Christ?

Balaam was a man of God. He heard from God and spoke as a prophet but he had a weakness tied to greed and covetousness. His weaknesses defiled his ministry. "Woe to them! For they have gone in the way of Cain, have run greedily in the error of Balaam for profit, and perished in the rebellion of Korah." (Jude 1:11) In Balaam, we see how we can live Godly lives in this modern world.

We live in a prosperous nation. We have everything at our fingertips, instant ordering, items delivered to our doors in one day or less. We are also all born into sin. We all are vulnerable to temptation because we are weak in our flesh. James says, "Blessed is the man who endures temptation; for when he has been approved, he will receive the crown of life which the Lord has promised to those who love Him." (James 1:12) For all of us, through Christ, by the Holy Spirit, by the Word of God, have the tools and capacity to overcome the temptation to hoard, to gather to ourselves, to be stingy and to be greedy.

> "Do not love the world or the things in the world. If anyone loves the world, the love of the Father is not in him. For all that is in the world—the lust of the flesh, the lust of the eyes, and the pride of life—is not of the Father but is of the world. And the world is passing away, and the lust of it; but he who does the will of God abides forever." (1 John 2:15-17)

In the Message version, we read:

> "Don't love the world's ways. Don't love the world's goods. Love of the world squeezes out

love for the Father. Practically everything that goes on in the world—wanting your own way, wanting everything for yourself, wanting to appear important—has nothing to do with the Father. It just isolates you from him. The world and all its wanting, wanting, wanting is on the way out—but whoever does what God wants is set for eternity."

We spend so much time wanting, reaching, grasping and pursuing things. In the kingdom of God, we find happiness and contentment in a person: Jesus Christ. In the kingdom of God, we can be filled with the person of Christ, and not the things of this world.

Our life, talents, time and money will be directed toward the things that are the most important to us. Jesus said for us to make sure it is heaven, God and the Kingdom of God. "Do not lay up for yourselves treasures on earth, where moth and rust destroy and where thieves break in and steal; but lay up for yourselves treasures in heaven, where neither moth nor rust destroys and where thieves do not break in and steal. For where your treasure is, there your heart will be also." (Matthew 6:19-21) That is what we should be seeking. God doesn't mind us having things, but he does mind things having us.

Covetousness and greed are things we must work to keep out of our lives, so that we stay out of the path that Balaam fell into. "They have forsaken the right way and gone astray, following the way of Balaam the son of Beor, who loved the wages of unrighteousness; but he was rebuked for his iniquity: a dumb donkey speaking with a man's voice restrained the madness of the prophet." It's one thing to error in life. It's another to keep committing that error as a chosen "way." A "way" means that we keep making the mistake by choice. Error is one thing. Sin is one thing, but letting it become a lifestyle is another thing. We have to work to make sure that sin does not become a lifestyle. Balaam didn't conquer his covetous heart. He was known as a man that could be bought off. The enemies of Israel paid him to detour the plan of God for Israel.

Here's the key: we build boundaries to constrain the sins in our lives so they don't become habits. We start by taking a stand not to allow sin to govern our lives. We decide that we aren't going to be bound by things anymore. We refuse to surrender. We resist the devil. We turn to God. If we don't, we are in danger of following Balaam's doctrine. "But I have a few things against you, because you have there those who hold the doctrine of Balaam, who taught Balak to put a stumbling block before the children of Israel, to eat things sacrificed to idols, and to commit sexual immorality." (Revelation 2:14) When people justify their sinful lifestyle, they are operating in the doctrine of Balaam. We meet people all of the time that do things that they used to view as sin, but now they justify their actions. This is most evident in couple sleeping together outside of marriage. It feels good to them. Why? The Holy Spirit has been so quenched by the chronic sinful act, He is no longer felt in a convicting way in their hearts.

Balaam's doctrine came about because he made an error and didn't stop there. His pattern of errors became a way that he traveled over and over again. He justified it and that became his doctrine. He didn't put up a boundary of contentment for himself.

So what does it mean to be content? First, it doesn't mean we can't have things.

"The ground of a certain rich man yielded plentifully. And he thought within himself, saying, 'What shall I do, since I have no room to store my crops?' So he said, 'I will do this: I will pull down my barns and build greater, and there I will store all my crops and my goods. And I will say to my soul, "Soul, you have many goods laid up for many years; take your ease; eat, drink, and be merry."' But God said to him, 'Fool! This night your soul will be required of you; then whose will those things be which you have provided?'

"So is he who lays up treasure for himself, and is not rich toward God." (Luke 12:16-21)

Looking at this parable of Christ, how many are in agreement with this? Can we be happy without a lot of stuff? The Bible doesn't say that wealth is bad. It says that wealth as the treasure of our heart, that is what is bad. There are two doctrines of treasure in the Bible: the doctrine of blessings and the doctrine of contentment. God wants us to have both: provision and contentment. He wants us to be happy in any state of life. It is vital to learn to be happy with no money in the bank or a lot of money in the bank.

Jesus shows us in this parable that it is okay to have stuff as long as God has access to our stuff. Whenever we keep things from God, He doesn't like that. Anything we can't give away owns us. We need to be rich in the things of God.

If someone is called to the mountain of business, and called to be an entrepreneur, God wants them to dream big. He also wants them to include in that dream how much they can give away before they die. It's not a sin to be a millionaire or a billionaire. The sin is to die with those millions or billions. We can't take it with us, but we can give it away. Contentment is an inside job. It is not easy but it is necessary.

Gilbert K. Chesterton said, "True contentment is a thing as active as agriculture. It is the power of getting out of any situation all that there is in it. It is arduous and it is rare." Contentment is the product of our choices and it is something we have to learn. " The Apostle Paul shows us that he had to learn to be content. So do we.

> But I rejoiced in the Lord greatly that now at last your care for me has flourished again; though you surely did care, but you lacked opportunity. Not that I speak in regard to need, for I have learned in whatever state I am, to be content: I know how to be abased, and I know how to abound. Everywhere and in all things I have learned both to be full and to be hungry, both to abound and to suffer need. I can do all things through Christ who strengthens me. (Philippians 4:10-13)

It is not born into us. We have to learn contentment. Our internal happiness and satisfaction doesn't rest on what is happening in our world. We can't wait to be happy. We can't postpone happiness for retirement. We can't put the weight of our happiness on things that can't fulfill us.

BUILDING A CONTENTMENT BOUNDARY

Jesus is the source of the strength we need to overcome the greed and covetousness that is hidden in our hearts. We can do all things through Christ.

"Now godliness with contentment is great gain. For we brought nothing into this world, and it is certain we can carry nothing out. And having food and clothing, with these we shall be content. But those who desire to be rich fall into temptation and a snare, and into many foolish and harmful lusts which drown men in destruction and perdition." (1 Timothy 6:6-9) The wealth our hearts truly desire is found in knowing God and in becoming like Christ. The wealthiest person in the world is the Christlike person. They are carrying in them the attributes of God. They find contentment in Him and they build a healthy boundary that helps them decide how much stuff they need.

There is no denying the fact that there is a thrill to buying something new. We get a high from it, much like a gambler gets during the game. We love getting the new car. But after six weeks, it gets old. The high goes away. Why? Things can't replace God in our lives. Things lose their prestige and meaning over time. Our appetite for things will never be filled. Paul is teaching us to be happy even if our car is not brand new or we live in an apartment or our clothes aren't trendy.

Greed stops people from being able to have peace and to be joyful. It keeps them from being grateful. The Bible gives us the remedy to Balaam's error, to the greed that is destroying our culture. This remedy, the principle of generosity, is also the way to grow in contentment. When we give things away, we kill off the greedy spirit that is ravaging our soul. It will kill off the need to have more. The need to hoard will die. When we give, we adopt the character of Christ and learn how to be content.

As we grow in our generosity, an amazing thing will happen: we will learn the great secret that we can't out-give God. Twice in our lives, Mary and I have given away all our possessions. I've given away twenty cars, two Rolex watches, and three entire sets of wardrobe. I love giving away stuff. I love to bless people. I love hearing God's voice and following His commands. I love being a part of His process of resourcing other people. I love to prove to God that stuff doesn't mean anything to me. But time and time again, He shows me that He can give me more than I can ever give away.

We don't have to live a greedy life. Giving is the way to conquer this sin. Contentment is being happy with what we have, and not unhappy with what we don't have. Can we be happy with the stuff we have now? If we can't, we have put our happiness in the power of an object and not in Jesus. We can be happy when we are single, married, with money, without money, at all times and in all places. Contentment focuses not on what we have, but who has us. Jesus can provide every need. He can give us wisdom in the realm of money that we never imagined. "Let your conduct be without covetousness; be content with such things as you have. For He Himself has said, "I will never leave you nor forsake you." (Hebrews 13:5)

Let's give God our hearts and allow Him to help us form a healthy boundary of contentment around it and begin to give sacrificially to His cause on the earth. Often the journey to generosity will begin with tithing. This Biblical principle, no matter what people say, was established four hundred years before the law of Moses. It is a strong cord running through the entire Bible. Whenever someone argues about tithing, they are justifying their behavior because they don't want to let God into their money. They don't do it because our sinful natures are cheap and selfish. We say that we've let God have our whole life, but then deny Him rule over our money. If He doesn't have your money, He doesn't have our heart. Often in our journey with Christ, the last thing to get saved is our wallets. The control of money has to be given up.

A FINAL WORD

Hear are some final thoughts on why we need the boundary of contentment in our hearts.

Discontent people are vulnerable to making bad decisions. They are constantly trying to satisfy their thirst.

Discontent people will always be unhappy and vulnerable to temptations.

And, finally, discontent people subject other people to rejection and dishonor. When someone is unhappy, they don't have a wall of contentment in their life. The people around them will feel responsible for their unhappiness.

CHAPTER SEVEN
THE POWER OF WORDS

*Words are singularly the most powerful force available
to humanity. We can choose to use this force constructively
with words of encouragement, or destructively using words of
despair. Words have energy and power with the ability to help,
to heal, to hinder, to hurt, to harm, to humiliate and to humble.*
- Yehuda Berg

*Death and life are in the power of the tongue,
And those who love it will eat its fruit.*
- Proverbs 18:21

God has not left us powerless. He gave us power in our
words. We have the choice to say things that are either
filled with life or death. God will never step into our
world and take possession of our mouth, so that we only
say perfect things. He's given us free will, free choice,
free moral agency. He tells us there is power in the
words we say. This allows us to overcome the handicap
of a negative vocabulary, but also to orchestrate God's
heavenly agenda here on the earth. We can say what

God wants to do in the earth, and it will be done. This is amazing but true: God can't do it until we say it.

When God made the universe and the natural dimension we live in, He didn't just think wonderful thoughts, and go about his business. God dreamed of things to create and then spoke those dreams into existence. He said what He thought. "By faith we understand that the worlds were framed by the word of God, so that the things which are seen were not made of things which are visible." (Hebrews 11:3) Our natural word is governed by the supernatural world He lives in. The rule of law in the spiritual world is the word of God. We have been given the glorious divine privilege, the inherited right, to create through our spoken word.

Let's work to become skillful kingdom agents and learn to speak things that are in-line with His thoughts and will. We can work to build God's kingdom in the earth with Him, by speaking what he says to us.

Here is a very plain fact: we can't be strong in our walk with God and have a weak vocabulary. It is God's will that we be strong in this world. No matter what, we have to speak His will out loud. Even if we have amazing encounters with God, where He reveals His truth to us, if we keep it to ourselves or we speak negative things in contrast, we limit Him working in our lives.

Very often, people outside of the church have recognized how powerful words are. This is the case with the centurion in Matthew 8:

> Now when Jesus had entered Capernaum, a centurion came to Him, pleading with Him, saying, "Lord, my servant is lying at home paralyzed, dreadfully tormented."

And Jesus said to him, "I will come and heal him."

The centurion answered and said, "Lord, I am not worthy that You should come under my roof. But only speak a word, and my servant will be healed. For I also am a man under authority, having soldiers under me. And I say to this one, 'Go,' and he goes; and to another, 'Come,' and he comes; and to my servant, 'Do this,' and he does it."

When Jesus heard it, He marveled, and said to those who followed, "Assuredly, I say to you, I have not found such great faith, not even in Israel! And I say to you that many will come from east and west, and sit down with Abraham, Isaac, and Jacob in the kingdom of heaven. But the sons of the kingdom will be cast out into outer darkness. There will be weeping and gnashing of teeth."

Then Jesus said to the centurion, "Go your way; and as you have believed, so let it be done for you." And his servant was healed that same hour. (Matthew 8:5-13)

When Jesus came into a city, people took notice. Even a Roman centurion, someone outside of Jesus' world. This man was unique, and he knew the power of the spoken word. He knew that if Jesus spoke, it would work for him, and do what it was meant to do. The centurion knew Jesus could only do on earth what heaven had given him authority to do. This military man had studied Jesus and realized that He was functioning like a military man. Orders passed down were carried out via the words spoken. He saw the similarities between the kingdoms—his and Jesus'. He knew that Jesus had power because He was under authority. He saw Jesus' words carrying out His will. He knew that we can have what we believe for if we speak it out. Our words have power.

A lot of us have been told that this type of belief is wrong. The "blab it and grab it" and "name it and claim it" group have done damage. I don't care about any of that. We need to know the truths in the Bible. The Bible says there is great consequence in the words we speak. I want to be a person that understands and takes advantage of the full force of our words.

If God is going to trust us with real power, we have to learn to govern our words. "For we all stumble in many things. If anyone does not stumble in word, he is a perfect man, able also to bridle the whole body. Indeed, we put bits in horses' mouths that they may obey us, and we turn their whole body. Look also at ships: although they are so large and are driven by fierce winds, they are turned by a very small rudder wherever the pilot desires. Even so the tongue is a little member and boasts great things." (James 3:2-5) James was a fierce warrior of righteousness. James knew the power of words. For us to be mature, for us to be able to handle power, we have to get a hold on what we say.

I love seeing horse trainers put tiny little seventy pound kids on horses and then watch that little child turn this massive beast —many times larger than the child's weight—with the bit and bridle. The horse responds to the instincts and tugs of the rider because his mouth has been trained. They follow wherever their mouth is being led. If we get a hold of our mouths, we can change the direction of our lives. "And none of us is perfectly qualified. We get it wrong nearly every time we open our mouths. If you could find someone whose speech was perfectly true, you'd have a perfect person, in perfect control of life. A bit in the mouth of a horse controls the whole horse. A small rudder on a huge ship in the hands of a skilled captain sets a course in the face of the strongest winds. A word out of your mouth may seem of no account, but it can accomplish nearly anything—or destroy it!" (James 3:2-5; The Message) Our spoken words can accomplish nearly anything. Our words can change this world that we live in.

RENEWING OUR LIVES

Bless the Lord, O my soul;
And all that is within me, bless His holy name!
Bless the Lord, O my soul,
And forget not all His benefits:
Who forgives all your iniquities,
Who heals all your diseases,
Who redeems your life from destruction,
Who crowns you with lovingkindness and
tender mercies,
Who satisfies your mouth with good things,
So that your youth is renewed like the eagle's.
(Psalm 103:1-5)

This psalm is a celebration of what God does for us. He forgives, heals, blesses and redeems. Often we overlook the last verse or we breeze over it. We shouldn't. In it is a powerful revelation: we can see restoration in our life by the words we say. One of the first things we have to fix to break out of a season of weakness is our speech.

Take a moment, and listen to what is coming out of your mouth, and decide if that is where you want to go in your life. What we say today will become concrete in our tomorrow.

If we spent as much time allowing God to satisfy our mouth with good things as we do saying things that are damaging or hurtful, our world would be a vastly different place. We have the restorative power of God in our mouths. Our words can improve our lives if we stop speaking dead things and start speaking God things.

Jesus, over forty times, used natural elements to speak the truth of God's will. Even in the discipleship of His men, He used the settings to teach them. In Mark 11, He teaches them the power of their words.

> Now the next day, when they had come out from Bethany, He was hungry. And seeing from afar a fig tree having leaves, He went to see if perhaps He would find something on it. When He came to it, He found nothing but leaves, for it was not the season for figs. In response Jesus said to it, "Let no one eat fruit from you ever again." And His disciples heard it…
>
> Now in the morning, as they passed by, they saw the fig tree dried up from the roots. And Peter, remembering, said to Him, "Rabbi, look! The fig tree which You cursed has withered away."
>
> So Jesus answered and said to them, "Have faith in God. For assuredly, I say to you, whoever says to this mountain, 'Be removed and be cast into the sea,' and does not doubt in his heart, but believes that those things he says will be done, he will have whatever he says. Therefore I say to you,

whatever things you ask when you pray, believe
that you receive them, and you will have them
(Mark 11:12-14, 20-24)

Jesus showed them that when we have faith, we talk
to stuff. We speak life into our marriages. We speak to
our car. We speak to our businesses. We dictate with our
words how things are going to be. He taught them that
faith filled words do amazing things. We will have what
we say. Whenever our faith is joined with our words, we
change the world.

"By faith we understand that the worlds were
framed by the word of God, so that the things
which are seen were not made of things which
are visible." (Hebrews 11:3)

THE POWER OF NAMING

Then they journeyed from Bethel. And when
there was but a little distance to go to Ephrath,
Rachel labored in childbirth, and she had hard
labor. Now it came to pass, when she was in hard
labor, that the midwife said to her, "Do not fear;
you will have this son also." And so it was, as her
soul was departing (for she died), that she called
his name Ben-Oni; but his father called him
Benjamin. (Genesis 35:16-18)

Rachel was advanced in years. She waited decades to
give birth to Joseph. As she gave birth to her second son,
her labor was bad. In the midst of it, tragedy struck. As

she died, Rachel's last breath was used to name her son. This godly woman, in the hall of faith, a person of great consequence, was so overtaken by grief, that she couldn't filter what she was saying. She couldn't stop her mouth. She called her son, Ben-oni, meaning the "son of my great sorrow." She basically said that her son child had killed her.

That would have been her child's name. He would have been known as the son that killed his mother, the son that caused sorrow. But Jacob took the child from the midwife and walked away. He knew the power of a bad name. He knew the power of words over a life. His name meant "heel grabber or con man." If we aren't careful, we will live up to what other's have said about us. If we don't watch out, the labels that people assign to us will become the defining marks of our lives.

Jacob refused to call him Ben-oni. He refused to allow a curse to define his last son. He called him Benjamin, "son of my right hand." There is a lot connected to that. We limit the work of God in people and places when we give the wrong name. When we name things in regards to how we see them, if the name is ungodly or off the mark, it will taint things. God responds, respects and honors things that we say.

God created the animals and paraded them before Adam. He asked Adam to name them. God called them whatever Adam called them. Adam was able to see their proper identities and name them correctly. The closer we are to God, the more correctly we label and name and call things. The Bible tells us that we have new names. Our identity has changed in Christ. We should be saying that we are the redeemed, the chosen, the children of God, the sons and daughters of God, the ambassadors of Christ.

DON'T GRIEVE THE HOLY SPIRIT

We should all take some time and examine what we are saying. Are we saying things that are at odds with God's will? Jesus wants us to start moving mountains. He wants us to start speaking to our mountains of difficulty. He is daring us to calculate our debt —all of it—and, everyday for the next thirty days, to say this, "In Jesus name, I am debt free." He is daring us to look at our mortgages and thank Jesus that our house is debt free. Something happens when we speak things out that agree with God's will. When we do that, we cooperate with the Holy Spirit and we stop grieving him.

> Therefore, putting away lying, "Let each one of you speak truth with his neighbor," for we are members of one another. "Be angry, and do not sin": do not let the sun go down on your wrath, nor give place to the devil. Let him who stole steal no longer, but rather let him labor, working with his hands what is good, that he may have something to give him who has need. Let no corrupt word proceed out of your mouth, but what is good for necessary edification, that it may impart grace to the hearers. And do not grieve the Holy Spirit of God, by whom you were sealed for the day of redemption. (Ephesians 4:25-30)

We can set boundaries around our lives by watching what we say and not give the devil a license to enter our lives.

The Holy Spirit can be quenched and grieved. We quench him by not doing what He wants us to do. We grieve Him by dong things He doesn't want us to do. The number one way the Holy Spirit is grieved in the earth is by peoples words. We want to have such a close relationship with the Holy Spirit that we are instantly bothered when we quench and grieve Him.

SETTING BOUNDARIES FOR OUR MOUTHS

There are some really simple ways to set up boundaries for our mouths and words. They are all based in questions that we can ask ourselves to establish what we believe and what we say to people.

1. Do we believe that words heal or hurt?
The power of life and death is in the words we say. Is what we say helping or hurting someone else? If our words aren't helping, they are almost always hurting. If what we say to someone doesn't help them, there is a really good chance it has added to their difficulties.

2. Are we meeting our own expectations?
Do we talk to others the way we want to be talked to and the way we want God to talk to us?

3. Is what you are saying in agreement with God and His word?
We saw this in Ephesians. We grieve the Holy Spirit when we say things that don't line up with God's will and Word.

4. Have I asked the Holy Spirit for help in guarding my mouth?

In the end, it will only be through the power of the Holy Spirit that we set boundaries around our mouths. "Set a guard, O Lord, over my mouth; Keep watch over the door of my lips." (Psalm 141:3) David prayed for God help David stop his mouth every time he was about to betray the will of God. David understood that what he said would come to pass immediately because of his earthly authority as king and due to the spiritual power of words. He prayed that his words would be guarded because he understood the real spiritual power of words.

CHAPTER EIGHT
FURTHER INGREDIENTS
FOR GODLY BOUNDARIES

*It's only by saying no that you can concentrate on the things
that really matter.*
- Scott Belsky

It is time to get our "No" back. We might feel overwhelmed by this life and the attacks launched against us, but hear the voice of God: "'Don't be afraid. Stand firm and watch God do his work of salvation for you today. Take a good look at the Egyptians today for you're never going to see them again.'" (Exodus 14:13)

God wants us to know that we have the power to say "no" to the sin, the relationship, the demonic attacks that have tormented us for a long time.

He wants us to erect Godly boundaries in our lives to keep damaging forces out.

He wants us all to know that when the devil comes with anxiety, sadness, depression and so on, we can say "no" to him.

We can't stop birds from flying over our heads, but we can stop them from making a nest in our hair. We can't stop the devil from attacking our lives, but we can stop him from coming in through the gates and into our houses, our minds, our wills and our emotions. God has given us elements to help us build Godly boundaries, a renewed thought life, a new nature, faith in Him and perseverance until He has finished working.

HIS PEACE

Be anxious for nothing, but in everything by prayer and supplication, with thanksgiving, let your requests be made known to God; and the peace of God, which surpasses all understanding, will guard your hearts and minds through Christ Jesus. Finally, brethren, whatever things are true, whatever things are noble, whatever things are just, whatever things are pure, whatever things are lovely, whatever things are of good report, if there is any virtue and if there is anything praiseworthy—meditate on these things. (Philippians 4:6-8)

Everything we pray about, everything we give to God, everything that we release to God, loses its grip and control over our life. Prayer is the way that we communicate with God and keep the walls up to keep the devil out. Prayer is where we share our hearts with Him. Prayer is the place where we unload stuff we aren't supposed to carry. It's our therapy session. It's out of these times with God, peace comes and acts as the guard or doorkeeper in our life. Peace determines what shouldn't be in us. Peace will become the governing force that determines what type of thoughts are allowed into our minds.

We have to do some work ourselves for peace to have its full effect in our lives. We need to get out the broom and sweep clean the things that have been dirtying our thought lives. It's time to brush out the old stinking thinking, and allow peace to control the areas that those thoughts used to control. The devil might send a thought, but we don't have to receive it. Everyone around us at work, in our families, in friendship circles, might be in upheaval, but we don't have to be. We can live with the opinions and feelings of others, but that doesn't mean we are ruled by them. We have the kingdom and peace of God ruling and governing our hearts. Our minds are safe and protected in the peace of God.

As peace takes over more of our thought life, we will find ourselves being careful and more attentive to what we expose ourselves to. Some of us are more sensitive than others. Because of the Internet and the massive amount of information on it, in minutes we can find something that offends, hurts, or depresses us. An act of terror may have happened around the world, and our whole day suddenly orbits around that sad event. God's peace can protect our minds.

RENEWED THOUGHT LIFE

"For as he thinks in his heart, so is he."
(Proverbs 23:7a)

As a man thinks...The word for "think", in the Hebrew, means "to estimate, to think, to reason." It means "to act as a gatekeeper." Whatever thoughts we allow into our belief system become words. Those words become deeds. The deeds become habits. Habits become character. And character determines our destiny. Everything starts with a thought.

An angry person doesn't have an anger fungus in their body. Wouldn't it be great if we could go to the doctor and get an anti-anger shot? An angry character starts with angry thoughts. People are angry because they never took control of their angry thoughts. Instead, those thoughts became angry words. The angry words became angry deeds. The angry deeds became habits, then character. We have the choice to either allow that angry thought to continue or we bring it to God and let him deal with it. "…casting down arguments and every high thing that exalts itself against the knowledge of God, bringing every thought into captivity to the obedience of Christ…" (2 Cor. 10:5) The act of taking our thoughts to God, applying His word to our minds, and processing it over and over again, leads to a renewed thought life. God, by His Word, by His Spirit, through Jesus, regains control of our minds and the boundary is formed.

THE NEW NATURE

Just because it happened, doesn't mean it has to happen again. One of the tricks the devil uses to pull people into unhealthy patterns of living is to tell them they can't stop doing something once they have gone through with it. Or that since something bad has happened once, it will happen again. These are lies. God is really good at helping us stop destructive life habits.

It may seem impossible at times because the longer something has gripped us, the stronger its controlling power seems to be. Jesus has given us a new nature, one that is full of the power of Christ to break the control of Satan. One that is on full display in Mark 9:

> Then one of the crowd answered and said, "Teacher, I brought You my son, who has a mute spirit. And wherever it seizes him, it throws him down; he foams at the mouth, gnashes his teeth, and becomes rigid. So I spoke to Your disciples, that they should cast it out, but they could not."
> He answered him and said, "O faithless generation, how long shall I be with you? How long shall I bear with you? Bring him to Me." Then they brought him to Him. And when he saw Him, immediately the spirit convulsed him, and he fell on the ground and wallowed, foaming at the mouth.
> So He asked his father, "How long has this been happening to him?"
> And he said, "From childhood. And often he has thrown him both into the fire and into the water to destroy him. But if You can do anything, have compassion on us and help us."
> Jesus said to him, "If you can believe, all things are possible to him who believes."
> Immediately the father of the child cried out and said with tears, "Lord, I believe; help my unbelief!"
> When Jesus saw that the people came running together, He rebuked the unclean spirit, saying to it: "Deaf and dumb spirit, I command you, come out of him and enter him no more!" Then the

spirit cried out, convulsed him greatly, and came
out of him. And he became as one dead, so that
many said, "He is dead." But Jesus took him by
the hand and lifted him up, and he arose. (Mark
9:17-27)

Like this little boy, all things are possible for us when
we believe. Things will change. We are not trapped
forever in our old nature. We can live the new life He
died to give us. The devil is not stronger than God.
Jesus will work in our lives to see us free. Just because
something bad hasn't happened yet, doesn't mean it
won't happen. Just because it keeps happening, doesn't
mean it will go on forever. God can break the grip of
anything in our lives. The key is to be honest. The father
in Mark 9 said that he believed, but he needed help in
his unbelief. We are all like this at times: we believe, yet
we struggle to believe at the same time.

Paul, in talking to the church at Ephesus, reminded
them of who they once were—liars, cheats, drunks. But
then he introduces them to their new nature.

This I say, therefore, and testify in the Lord,
that you should no longer walk as the rest of the
Gentiles walk, in the futility of their mind, having
their understanding darkened, being alienated
from the life of God, because of the ignorance
that is in them, because of the blindness of
their heart; who, being past feeling, have
given themselves over to lewdness, to work all
uncleanness with greediness.

But you have not so learned Christ, if indeed
you have heard Him and have been taught by

Him, as the truth is in Jesus: that you put off, concerning your former conduct, the old man which grows corrupt according to the deceitful lusts, and be renewed in the spirit of your mind, and that you put on the new man which was created according to God, in true righteousness and holiness. (Ephesians 4:17-24)

There comes a time when the Holy Spirit will speak to us about a pattern or an issue in our life, and He will say, "No more." The father in Mark chapter nine was desperate. He wanted his son to be saved from the spirit that was trying to kill him. Though it had been happening for a long time, the time had come and Jesus said, "No more." Someone out there right now is hearing this word and I want to say to them: it is time for the torment to end. "NO MORE!"

I pray that God gives all of us faith to believe and say, "NO MORE" for those things we have long prayed for. I believe Jesus is stepping into those situations and saying, "NO MORE!" It's time for that oppression or addiction or tormenting thought to stop. It's time for the boundary of the new nature to stand tall and keep those things out. Let's allow God to grow our faith to the point that we say, "NO MORE!" It doesn't matter how long it has lasted. The time has come for that thing, that debt, that sickness, that mental illness to end. "NO MORE!"

FAITH IN HIM

Just because someone said it, doesn't mean you have to believe it. In Mark 5 we have the story of Jairus. As Jesus is walking with him to his house, a messenger runs up.

While He was still speaking, some came from the ruler of the synagogue's house who said, "Your daughter is dead. Why trouble the Teacher any further?"

As soon as Jesus heard the word that was spoken, He said to the ruler of the synagogue, "Do not be afraid; only believe." And He permitted no one to follow Him except Peter, James, and John the brother of James. Then He came to the house of the ruler of the synagogue, and saw a tumult and those who wept and wailed loudly. When He came in, He said to them, "Why make this commotion and weep? The child is not dead, but sleeping."

And they ridiculed Him. But when He had put them all outside, He took the father and the mother of the child, and those who were with Him, and entered where the child was lying. Then He took the child by the hand, and said to her, "Talitha, cumi," which is translated, "Little girl, I say to you, arise."

Immediately the girl arose and walked, for she was twelve years of age. And they were overcome with great amazement. But He commanded them strictly that no one should know it, and said that something should be given her to eat. (Mark 5:35-43)

The second part of the message to Jairus was full of psychological warfare from the devil. Jairus was desperate. He went where others in his position wouldn't have gone —to Jesus. And the devil wanted to make sure he paid for it and never turned to Jesus again. So he sent a messenger to him saying the daughter was dead and that Jesus didn't need to come.

Jesus immediately said to Jairus that faith was the only thing Jarius should have in his mind. The outcome of this story was based on Jarius believing Jesus's words over the word from his house. It was not too late for God to do anything. Jairus hung on to Jesus' words. With Jesus nothing is ever beyond hope.

Whatever we are hoping for God to do in our lives, it doesn't matter what others think or if they say it's too late or that it is over. Jesus is saying the opposite. It's never too late. It will happen. It isn't over. It is worth the time we spend in prayer, it is worth the hours of waiting, it is worth the mental effort to change our thought life. Whatever we are praying for, we can't let other people talk us out of it. If God has moved on our heart to pray for it, we can't let go of it.

This generation is becoming more antagonistic to Christ. If we aren't careful, the devil will use the media, friends, family, co-workers to launch doubt and fear, in the hope of stealing His Words from our heart. Faith is a heart thing. We are never to be afraid of what others are saying. God will do what He said He would do.

Our story isn't over. We are not finished. If a marriage is being shaken, don't give up. Don't believe it when people say things can't work out.

If your business is on the rocks, don't give up. If someone is trying to start a new company, keep going. I am a serial, kingdom entrepreneur. I love to start things in and out of my church. We have launched a few new campuses out of our church lately. I'm now starting to look at other states and countries to start more things. Whenever I do this, there are always more against me than for me. They throw up the costs and the obstacles. But I can't help it. I have faith. I'm not going to let someone talk my mind out of my heart's faith.

No one could talk Jesus out of His destiny. Jesus was very clear regarding what He was about to do, but his own men couldn't hear it. They had a perception of what he was saying that was very different from what He said. They couldn't see the plan of God.

> From that time Jesus began to show to His disciples that He must go to Jerusalem, and suffer many things from the elders and chief priests and scribes, and be killed, and be raised the third day.
> Then Peter took Him aside and began to rebuke Him, saying, "Far be it from You, Lord; this shall not happen to You!"
> But He turned and said to Peter, "Get behind Me, Satan! You are an offense to Me, for you are not mindful of the things of God, but the things of men." (Matthew 16:21-23)

Peter, representing the other eleven, spoke out of fear, not faith. Jesus recognized that the devil was using someone very close to Him to try and stop the destiny God had for Him. He stayed in faith, knowing that God was going to use Him, and He spoke to that voice and told it to shut up.

PERSEVERING UNTIL HE IS DONE

Just because it didn't happen then, doesn't mean it won't happen now. The traditional definition of insanity is doing the same thing over and over and expecting different results. But I refute that. Sometimes you have to do the same thing over and over before it works for you. Sometimes, we have to keep pushing something through if God wants it to be done. Just because something doesn't happen fast, or the first time, doesn't mean it won't happen now.

> So it was, as the multitude pressed about Him to hear the word of God, that He stood by the Lake of Gennesaret, and saw two boats standing by the lake; but the fishermen had gone from them and were washing their nets. Then He got into one of the boats, which was Simon's, and asked him to put out a little from the land. And He sat down and taught the multitudes from the boat.
> When He had stopped speaking, He said to Simon, "Launch out into the deep and let down your nets for a catch."
> But Simon answered and said to Him, "Master, we have toiled all night and caught nothing; nevertheless at Your word I will let down the net."
> 6 And when they had done this, they caught a great number of fish, and their net was breaking. (Luke 5:1-6)

In the unfruitful areas of life, we have nothing to lose by bringing Jesus into that area. Jesus tells professional fisherman to go back out and to fish in the middle of the day. This was the wrong time of day to fish and Peter knew it. Peter's first response was to give Jesus the facts, but as Peter talked, we see that his faith in God trumped the facts he faced. They had a fruitless night and now at the wrong time, Jesus was telling them to try again. Peter was conflicted. Faith was fighting doubt, fear and logic. In that moment, he learned that faith comes even when there is doubt in our lives. Faith is the moment when we trust God enough to act in spite of our doubts.

Despite the fear and doubt, Peter did act on Jesus' word. A carpenter and prophet told him, a fisherman, what to do and Peter acted on it. When we act on faith despite the fear, logic, circumstance, doctors, diagnosis, facts, God meets us there. Peter's mind might have said it wouldn't work, but his spirit said it would. Faith changes facts, and "they caught a great number of fish, and their net was breaking." Their season of fruitlessness ended immediately. Our seasons of fruitlessness is going to end. The enemy will try to steal opportunities from us by convincing us that old patterns, old ways and old examples are the future. That is a lie.

I want to ask you, what would life be like if we expected success, miracles and favor? We could go over all the old areas of life where we experienced pain, loss, fruitlessness and barrenness and watch as God turned it all around for us.

God can make the most unhealthy marriage the best marriage. God can touch a business that looks hopeless and show the world what the kingdom of God looks like in that sphere.

In Psalm 42, David poured out his frustration because he knew that just because God's promise hadn't happened yet in his life, didn't mean it wouldn't happen soon.

As the deer pants for the water brooks,
So pants my soul for You, O God.
My soul thirsts for God, for the living God.
When shall I come and appear before God?
My tears have been my food day and night,
While they continually say to me,
"Where is your God?"
When I remember these things,
I pour out my soul within me.
For I used to go with the multitude;
I went with them to the house of God,
With the voice of joy and praise,
With a multitude that kept a pilgrim feast.
Why are you cast down, O my soul?
And why are you disquieted within me?
Hope in God, for I shall yet praise Him
For the help of His countenance.
O my God, my soul is cast down within me;
Therefore I will remember You from the land of
the Jordan,
And from the heights of Hermon,
From the Hill Mizar.
Deep calls unto deep at the noise of Your
waterfalls;
All Your waves and billows have gone over me.
The Lord will command His lovingkindness in
the daytime,
And in the night His song shall be with me—
A prayer to the God of my life.
I will say to God my Rock,
"Why have You forgotten me?
Why do I go mourning because of the
oppression of the enemy?"

As with a breaking of my bones,
 My enemies reproach me,
 While they say to me all day long,
"Where is your God?"
 Why are you cast down, O my soul?
 And why are you disquieted within me?
 Hope in God;
 For I shall yet praise Him,
 The help of my countenance and my God.

We can't give up because it hasn't happened yet. We can't let go just because we haven't seen God do it yet. Let's stand with Christ, "and let us not grow weary while doing good, for in due season we shall reap if we do not lose heart." (Galatians 6:9)

DR. MICHAEL & MARY MAIDEN

Dr. Michael Maiden and Mary, his beloved wife of over 35 years, are the senior pastors of Church for the Nations in Phoenix, Arizona. Here he strongly and lovingly prepares God's people for service in God's Kingdom. The messages are always relevant, timely and life-changing as well as prophetic.

Dr. Maiden has earned both a Masters and Doctorate Degree in Christian Psychology. He has authored seven books including: The Joshua Generation: God's Manifesto for the End Time Church, and his most recent book, Turn the World Upside Down, which speaks to this present generation about the next step to be taken.

In addition to his work in the local church, he is a strong prophetic voice to this generation and has ministered to those holding Public Offices as well as Pastors and Ministers throughout the world. Dr. Maiden is President and CEO of Church On The Rock International – a dynamic ministry that oversees more than 6,000 churches worldwide. He is also on the board of Fishers of Men International, the Jewish Voice International and several local churches.

To order books and materials from Dr. Michael Maiden, visit:

http://www.michaelmaiden.info